THE DAY NINA SIMONE STOPPED SINGING

THE DAY NINA SIMONE STOPPED SINGING

Darina Al-Joundi
with Mohamed Kacimi

Translated from the French by Marjolijn de Jager

THE FEMINIST PRESS
AT THE CITY UNIVERSITY OF NEW YORK
FEMINISTPRESS.ORG

Published in 2011 by the Feminist Press
at the City University of New York
The Graduate Center
365 Fifth Avenue, Suite 5406
New York, NY 10016

feministpress.org

Translation copyright © 2011 by Marjolijn de Jager
Originally published as *Le jour où Nina Simone a cessé de chanter*.
Copyright © 2008 by Actes Sud

 This project is supported in part by an award from
the National Endowment for the Arts.

Cover design by Faith Hutchinson
Cover photo by Dorothée Thébert Filliger
Text design by Drew Stevens

Library of Congress Cataloging-in-Publication Data

Al-Joundi, Darina, 1968–
[Jour où Nina Simone a cessé de chanter. English.]
The day Nina Simone stopped singing / by Darina Al-Joundi, with Mohamed
Kacimi ; translated from the French by Marjolijn de Jager.
    p. cm.
ISBN 978-1-55861-683-7
1. Al-Joundi, Darina, 1968– 2. Lebanon—History—Civil War,
1975–1990—Personal narratives. I. Kacimi, Mohamed, 1955–
II. Title.
DS87.5.J6813 2011
956.9204'4092--dc22
[B]
                                                    2010050136

FOREWORD

IN JUNE 2006, I WAS ORGANIZING AN EVENT AROUND the issue of Beirut in a theater in Paris. At the end of the performance a shy young woman, frightened even, and dressed in black, approached, handed me a manuscript, and then disappeared without saying a word. I read it that same evening. It was an open letter to her father who had dreamed of the greatest of freedoms for his daughter while she, precisely because of this freedom, would come to know the worst servility. The text was circumspect, metaphoric. I phoned her to find out whether she was prepared to take it any further, to disclose everything fully. She welcomed the opportunity with extraordinary openness. She told me the story of her childhood, her wars, her drug habit, and her love affairs without any self-censorship. She talked, I wrote. This encounter gave birth to a deep friendship and a play that I submitted to Alain Timar, the director of the Théâtre des Halles in Avignon. The following day, he took the TGV to Paris to propose to her that it be put on at the Festival of Avignon where he would be happy to welcome her. She had been an actress since the age of eight but had never performed in France. Her exile from Lebanon had cut her off from the stage. She was so eager to perform. From the third day on the public was already fighting to see her. Irreverent, beautiful, passionate, and liberated, she was worth her weight in gold in the Chapelle Sainte-Claire.

The entire national press reported on her performance. Laure Adler and Fabienne Pascaud wrote that she was the revelation of the 2007 festival. The fairy tale continued. Thierry Fabre, who had seen the show, asked us to write an account of it. Back in Paris, Darina described her life to me day after day, sometimes in Arabic, sometimes in French, taking it year by year, and I wrote. In the end, I had hundreds of sheets of paper. I needed to piece it together without ever losing the music of her oral story, to make it into a fiction in which everything is true. Darina's biography recounts the lunacy of Lebanon's history as well, that same Lebanon that rejoices in times of war and falls apart in times of peace, in the same way that it tells of the vulnerability of women's freedom, which in the eyes of men shall forever remain a foreign language.

MOHAMED KACIMI

1

"STOP WITH THAT WRETCHED KORAN!"

I don't know why I screamed. But I had to scream so that I wouldn't break the promise I had made to my father not to have the Koran read at his funeral.

My father died the day he knew that he had no further stories to tell me. I stand before his remains. In the middle of the large room he is naked beneath a simple white shroud. Lying on his back, his hands are folded over his genitals. I look at him. He looks so serene. It is the first time in my life that I feel he is at peace. I am not sorry he is dead. I've known for a long time that he was going to die because he had told me everything. Through the open window I see the houses of my village, Arnoun, which they used to call the Château de Beaufort. The bombed-out houses are still smoking. After a twenty-year occupation, the Israeli army has just evacuated southern Lebanon. I see the surrounding hills, dark with people. They have come from Tyr, Sidon, Damascus, Aleppo, Beirut, and Amman to attend my father's funeral. I caress his face: his skin is like a baby's, not even cold. It is January. It's raining. I can smell the rain as it surfaces from the red soil of southern Lebanon. In the distance I see the plains of Galilee, and high up there I watch the snow falling slowly on the peaks of Mount Hermon. The door opens. Women in black appear. They are weeping and moaning. They throw themselves on my father. They kiss his face. They kiss his hands. They kiss his feet so fervently! I whisper in my father's ear, "You bastard, one can always rely on you."

Suddenly I heard a strange voice that ripped through me. An intolerable cry that split my skull, pierced my skin: someone was wailing verses from the Koran. I flung open the door to the next room. It was filled with women in black weeping around a cassette player broadcasting prayers. I stepped over and on them, snatched the cassette player, and shut it off. The women shouted out in horror. My mother and my sisters tried to grab hold of me, shouting, "Stop that! You're mad! Come back, this is not the time . . . "

I ran to hide in my father's room and double-locked the heavy oak door. I heard the men hollering, "You crazy woman, give back the Koran or we'll kill you. Open up, you bitch, open up! One doesn't cut off the voice of God. Open up, you bitch, if you so much as touch God's Book you're dead."

From behind the door I yelled back, "This God is not my father's God! My father never had a God. He made me swear, 'Daughter of mine, watch out that those dogs don't use the Koran the day I die. Daughter of mine, I beg you, I would like some jazz at my death, and even some hip-hop, but definitely no Koran.' I'll be glad to play Nina Simone for him, Miles Davis, Fairouz, and even Mireille Mathieu, but no Koran. Do you hear me, I'll play *Last Tango in Paris* for him instead of your prayers. He loved La Coupole and butter, Papa did. He always used slightly salted Fleurier. You won't bury him like this. You won't get it back. I'll never open up for you."

I took out the cassette of the Koran and replaced it with Nina Simone's "Save Me." The pounding on the door became even louder. And I was dancing, alone, in front of my father. I was speaking to him, loudly, as if I wanted to awaken him from his death, "Happy now? You got your Nina Simone, you got your jazz. I spared you from the Koran, didn't I? And now what am I going to do? Who will protect me from these monsters? You were the one who taught me, 'Watch out, my girl, all the men in this country are monstrous to women. They're obsessed with appearances, they're tethered to the customs, they're eroded by God, they're gobbled up by their mothers, they're agitated about money, they spend their lives offering their asses to God on a platter, they open their flies the way you arm a submachine gun, they turn their sex organs loose on women the way you turn a pit bull loose. They're dogs!'"

Just now, one of your former mistresses wanted to kiss your hands. I suggested that she kiss your cock instead. You never know, she might have been able to resuscitate you. She could have played Jesus to your Lazarus.

2 AS A CHILD I USED TO BITE EVERYONE. MY sister Nayla still has my tooth marks on her body. I hated dressing like a girl. I wore my hair cut very short. I had the face of a little thug. The villagers called me "little Hassan," they were convinced I was a boy. I despised washing myself because it was so cold. I was dirty because I chased after grasshoppers that I'd put in matchboxes after first breaking their legs. I made them into salads that I served to the children of the village of Arnoun.

Our house was built of stones from the Château de Beaufort, an eleventh-century fortress constructed by the crusaders. It controlled the Palestine road. The house stood apart from the rest of the village, the road leading there lined with linden trees and weeping willows. The soil of the surrounding fields is bloodred, covered with huge sunflowers and chunks of white clay that look like sculptures of a mythical bestiary.

My father was an odd bird. He was born in 1933 in Salamiyeh, a town in northern Syria where poets, writers, and Communists lived. Most of its inhabitants are Ismailites, a Neoplatonic sect for whom reason takes precedence over faith. The Ismailites have a temple where they pray to Aristotle and Plato instead of Jesus and Mohammed.

In 1958, when he was twenty-five, my father went into exile in Lebanon where he taught literature and philosophy, first in Tyr, then in Beirut. During his lifetime he never lost his Salamiyeh accent. He always wore an abaya and open leather sandals that his mother sent him, together with a box of cakes, from Syria each year on the day of the Eid. He had met my mother in Beirut. Her pregnancy soon followed and they were forced to marry to avoid a scandal.

My mother was one of the great names in Lebanese radio. She came from a large family of well-educated landowners, with a father who was an officer in the gendarmerie. He had served in the army of Sharif Hussein of Jordan, who had entrusted his last flag to him. My grandfather kept it in the tall armoire in his room. On it the Sharif had written, "This flag will go to the one who will liberate Jerusalem one day." As children we believed that Palestine was a fairy tale.

Since my grandfather never finished anything he began, the bathroom had remained roofless. I took my showers in the sun or under the star-studded sky. In the fields there was a basin in which rainwater was collected. No one in the South had any running water.

My grandmother came from a family of landowners from Ghandouriyeh. She had property on the banks of the Litani, where we spent our vacations. She had never worn a veil. At that time there wasn't a woman anywhere in the South who wore one and no one celebrated Ramadan.

At dusk I would often visit the ruins of the Château de Beaufort with my father. He insisted that the place was haunted by a knight looking for his mistress, who was dressed in a voluminous blue gown. I believed him so completely that I could hear the lovers kiss in the dark.

At the time, my father had a blue Simca, worked at the newspaper *Le Destour* in Beirut, and taught at the orthodox school. He loved drinking, listening to music, and surrounding himself with women. He was extremely attached to Arnoun, which reminded him of Salamiyeh, the village where he was born. We used to get up early.

Khadidja the housekeeper would knock on the door at dawn. She'd make pancakes with a fine batter, sugar, and butter. I'd take the pot to go get milk at the neighbor's house, and when I returned the table would be covered with olives, farmer cheese, tomatoes that smelled like summer, cucumbers, and above all baskets of prickly pears that used to give me incredible constipation.

We were three sisters but Rana, the eldest, was very distant from us from the start. She wrote poems and was very close to grandfather whose side she never left. I was too mean and my sister Nayla was too sweet. I used to stuff peas up her nostrils, and serve her fruit full of worms. She trusted me. She swallowed it all with her eyes closed.

Rather than lecturing me my father was delighted with my foolish actions. He had a barbaric enthusiasm for all my mischief. I think that from our childhood on he refused to play the father role, so he could be party to our mistakes, our transgressions, and our success. To teach us Arabic he would sing us songs from Salami-yeh at six o'clock in the morning; he loved for us to get up early. Even on the john he would respond to us in poetry. He had written one volume of poetry on ciga-rette packs during a stay in prison in Syria. He would recite lines from them when he wasn't turning up Maria Callas before launching loudly into Arabic drinking songs. He worshipped Mahmoud Darwich and loathed Adonis who had never criticized the dictatorship of the Alaouite regime of Damascus. He spent whole evenings evoking the glory of the Omeyyades or the Abassides before sporadically starting in on dialectical materialism. He assured us that Marx was born in Salamiyeh.

As the sun set my parents would settle down beneath a trellis that almost formed a tent and provided an amazing amount of shade. We had a wooden table covered with a yellow oilcloth. They'd play cards and drink arrack. My father smoked heavily, five packs of Gitanes a day. He'd drop his ashes everywhere and the carpets in our house were littered with them. My mother was very much in love with him. She knew he had many affairs but pretended not to know anything about them.

Our childhood was a constant feast. Our parents taught us the meaning of beauty. Poets, journalists, activists would knock on our door spontaneously at any hour of the day or night. My mother was always improvising. In a flash she'd have the table set for twenty people. Appetizers, grilled meats, stuffed vine leaves, kibbe, cheeses, chicken wings, and falafel would miraculously flood the table. Alcohol flowed freely. As children we'd often sleep under the table not to miss a single poem.

My childhood was a perpetual clinking of arrack glasses and my father's laughter shaking the walls.

3 BEIRUT WAS A FREE CITY, THE OASIS OF EVERY Arab intellectual who in his own country was forced into silence. It was also the capital of the PLO, the Palestinians made the laws, and Beirut was their republic. Beirut was a brothel, too, with the whores from Hamra and from the harbor who'd walk the streets in the area of Saint-Georges. My father spent his life between the Dolce Vita in Raouché and the Horse Shoe in Hamra. He taught in the morning, spent his early evenings editing the newspaper, and finished his nights by drinking and dancing at the Uncle Sam, the Cave des Rois, or the Whisky à Gogo. It was la dolce vita. He would always go out with my mother, and together they'd live it up. He never hid his wife the way most Arabs do. He wrote thirteen novels and all his poems on café terraces.

I was born on February 25, 1968 in Beirut, but my father wasn't there the day I was born. He'd just gone underground to "liberate Palestine." I do remember his return. I was in my room, I had just turned three, I see a rather tall man, with large blue eyes, and a beginning baldness; he throws himself at me and I run off in tears. It was my father, and he would never forget this first encounter. We, my parents and my two sisters and I, lived in a large house in Ain-el-Roumaneh, right in the heart of the Christian quarter.

My father was a fervently secular man. Throughout his life he made sure to live only in Christian quarters and to have us educated only in Catholic schools. He admired Christ, compared him to Che Guevara. He thought he was handsome and said that a man who can change water into wine can't be all bad.

When I was five, my father registered me at the School of the Holy Family with the nuns in the Baabda quarter. He never told me whether I was Christian or Muslim. I loved going to the school chapel, the scent of incense intoxicated me, and I never missed the masses in classic Arabic and Latin. I loved the vision of the Christian Lebanese women when they entered a church: they would throw themselves so covetously on Christ's statue. They'd grasp his hips and cover him with noisy kisses from his knees to his chest. They'd lick his navel and glory in his thighs. I, in turn, learned how to grasp Christ by the waist and kiss his loincloth. I was becoming a true Maronite.

At school we were strictly forbidden to speak Arabic in class and at recess. During the first hour, the nuns would hand out sticks known as "signs." As soon as a child said one word in Arabic, an informer would slip one of those "signs" into that kid's pocket. At the end of the day, the nuns would count the number of infractions committed in our mother tongue and punish us. Being a disorderly pupil, I was forced to copy "I will never speak Arabic" hundreds of times each day.

I didn't like the French or math classes, but I was fanatic about catechism. I swallowed the Host by the handfuls and let myself be rocked like a baby by the stories of Mary Magdalene, Lazarus, Judas, and the miraculous draft of fishes. I was thrilled when Sister Marie told us the story of Jesus and the prostitute. Beirut was a city of hookers and I imagined them all kissing Christ for having spared them from being stoned.

I SUCKED MY THUMB ALL THE TIME AND PLAYED WITH my belly button. My mother tried everything but to no avail. One evening, she put a sheet over her head and burst into our room. I broke up with laughter but my older sister peed on herself. Rana was very authoritative. One day when she was on the swing I begged her to let me have a turn. She refused. I picked up a big stone. She looked at me threateningly and said, "Strike if you're a man!"

I struck her very hard. She ended up with five stitches on her forehead.

Nayla and I would sing all the time. My father used us as a jukebox when his friends were over in the evening. He very frequently took us out. It was with him that I discovered the theater, very early on, when we went to see the most popular actor of the time, Chouchou, play at the Grand Theater of Beirut. He had a very long mustache like Father Vassiliu. One night, I slipped into his box. I just wanted to pull at his mustache to see if it was real but the guards thwarted my plan.

One day at Holy Family, I made a stupid bet with my girlfriends that I would lift Sister Marie-Thérèse's blue dress at the moment that she'd bend over the altar in the chapel to light the candles. I did. To punish me she crushed cheese on my neck, face, hands, and legs before locking me up in a tiny unlit cell. She said, "You'll see, little heathen, the rats will come and devour you from head to toe."

I wasn't afraid. Strengthened by my catechism I told myself that if the rats should ever attack me, Jesus would come to stone them.

4 IN 1975, MY GRANDPARENTS DECIDED TO MOVE into the same building where we had a large apartment that looked out over enormous orchards.

My paternal grandmother, who was Syrian, spent most of her time at our place. She had just turned seventy. She could spend hours on end rubbing her hair with olive oil. Her chest was unusually bountiful. All I wanted was to see her breasts. One summer afternoon she'd gone off to take her bath. It was now or never. I opened the door abruptly. She was naked, standing in the bathtub, her hair all black, her pubis all white, her skin rippling in endless rolls of fat. And her astonishing breasts, like filled goatskins, with aureolae as wide as oranges, came tumbling down to her waist. I shut the door and shrieked, "Grandma has cow's breasts, grandma has cow's breasts."

I was given the first spanking of my life.

OUR EVENINGS WERE SPENT BETWEEN HAMRA AND the coastal road, the beaches at Saint-Georges and those at Saint-Simon. We would eat ice cream at the Place des Canons and falafel at Sayoune, see movies at the Rivoli Theater and have chocolate at Wimpy's. In Hamra every poet, every writer had his own table and would be surrounded by his devotees. Some would lecture the others or offer them drinks. My father couldn't live without going out or having something festive on the program. He had to be continually creating an event, or fabricating some reason to invite his friends. The riskiest moments involved going home. He used to drink a lot and he insisted on being the only one driving.

True, life was beautiful, but from very early on my sisters and I were aware that we were not like the rest. Our father was a political refugee from Syria, with just a simple residence permit that had to be renewed every three months and, because of the law that exists in every Arab country, our Lebanese mother could not transfer her nationality to us because she was a woman. All three of us were undocumented in the land of our birth. And in Lebanon, where all people exist solely through their community and their faith, we had neither. We didn't know whether we were Christian or Muslim.

When we would ask our father the question, he'd answer, "You are liberated girls. Period."

After my grandmother's breasts I acquired a passion for boys' testicles. Their texture fascinated me as much as the folds that looked like corduroy, those things that were sometimes soft, hanging down like rotten fruit, sometimes distended and growing smooth like pumice stone. I wanted to discover their secret. I got my chance one day when one of my young cousins came to spend the night. He must have been about eight. With no forewarning, I dragged him into my room when everyone was asleep and pulled down his pants. When I saw his genitals I felt something like a ravenous hunger. I wanted to press his balls like a bunch of grapes, not to hurt him but out of pure gluttony, the same as wanting to knead a soft caramel candy. I squeezed the object of my desire with all my might. He let out a scream that woke up the entire building.

The evening of my eighth birthday, February 25, 1976, my father was waiting for me at home alone. My mother was still at the radio station. He put on a Nina Simone record, "Feeling Good." He lit a candle, stuck in a Ballantine bottle. He asked me to sit down opposite him. He took out two crystal glasses and then a bottle of Bordeaux, a Pessac-Léognan. He looked as serious as if he were at mass. Very slowly he served me my first glass of wine before he spoke, "Dardoura, my daughter, you are a big girl now. It's time to start enjoying the real pleasures of life."

I raised my glass to his health. I drank. I felt the warmth in my belly. I looked at my father's blue eyes that gleamed as they never had before, I looked at the flame dancing and seemingly growing larger and larger. I listened to Nina Simone. Through the open window I saw the snow-tipped mountain, and I felt I was rising very high into the sky of Beirut.

"Well, my girl," he asked, "How do you feel?"

"I feel higher than the sky, Papa."

"Bravo, you've grasped the true destination of Bordeaux."

He served me several glasses. In the end everything was spinning inside my head, the mountain, his eyes, the candle, and Nina Simone above all. I was stumbling over my words and he, across from me, was doubled over with laughter. I couldn't speak anymore. My hand was shaking. I was looking for a glass of water but couldn't manage to get hold of it. My father was laughing like a child at my intoxication. Suddenly the door opened. My grandfather, a religious man, saw the scene. He picked me up to take me to the toilet and let me vomit. He shouted at my father, "You're mad, not only are you an atheist but now you want to turn your daughters into hookers, too. You're teaching them how to get drunk, have you no shame!"

Still uproarious, my father let fly, "I'm not making them into hookers, Grandpa, I'm making liberated women of them."

5 ZEÏNA, A WOMAN FROM SOUTHERN PALESTINE, came to clean our house every morning. She was a young girl with very long dark curly hair. Early in April 1975 she would often arrive looking very pale and she'd be shaking while she swept the floor. One day she suddenly appeared in tears and told my father that she couldn't come to us anymore in the East.

My father asked her what was going on. It turned out that the young Phalangists who loitered in front of our building every morning cursed and threw stones at her, yelling, "Go home, you dirty Arab."

My father was beside himself, "Oh, yes, I can see them from here, those Swedes who treat the Palestinians like dirt. They'll pay dearly for it some day."

Zeïna left the very same day.

Most Lebanese Christian families say they're descendants of the Phoenicians. This prestigious mythic and mythological ancestry precludes them from being related to the Arabs, a definition they reserve for people of "lower extraction" such as the Syrians or the Palestinians, whom they loathe.

April 13, 1975 was a Sunday. My mother was working at the radio station. I heard her voice as she was broadcasting. My father raised the volume on the radio, which announced that the activists of the National Party of Syria had killed Pierre Gemayel's bodyguard during the inauguration of a church in West Beirut.

The whole family came together for the meal. It was hot. I went upstairs to my grandmother's on the sixth floor.

She had prepared a dish of *labné mkaazalée*, which is *fromage frais* marinated in olive oil. I was on the balcony, juggling little balls of cheese in the air when I saw people running in every direction. Gunshots were fired, men were dashing toward the orchards. My mother came running home from work holding a box of pastries. She'd stopped at the Ain-el-Roumaneh Bridge, she'd seen the Phalangists block a bus full of Palestinians, make them get off, and then slaughter them one by one. I was numb, didn't understand, kept tossing my cheese balls in the air when one of them fell on the head of a militiaman who then looked up at the balcony and showered me with obscenities. That was the day the war began.

The following morning I arrived at Holy Family, just like every other morning. I'd forgotten the scenes of the previous evening. When I was supposed to go to the chapel for my catechism class at four o'clock, Sister Marie-Thérèse stopped me, "Where are you off to, just like that?"

"To catechism, Sister!"

"What are you?"

I didn't understand. I'd never asked myself the question, nor had my parents. I was dumbfounded. The nun was very much on edge.

"I don't know, Sister," I answered.

She was surprised by my response, completely taken aback really.

"What do you mean you don't know what you are? Didn't your parents tell you anything?"

"Tell me what, Sister?"

"Where you come from."

My face lit up, I was beginning to get it.

"Yes, of course, I'm from Beirut."

"That's not what I'm talking about. Surely they must have told you to what Church you belong."

I nodded my head, no.

She felt sorry for me.

"Are they dead? Are they deaf-mutes?"

"No, Sister, they talk, they're alive."

Only then did I understand that I really was a hieroglyph in the eyes of the good sister, who now began to shout, "What do you mean you don't know? You're in Lebanon, we all know where we come from, to what community we belong, of which there are seventeen in our country; so are you Armenian, Greek Orthodox, Greek Catholic, Eastern Orthodox, Maronite? Even cats know to what religion their families belong, even a dog can smell whether his leash is held by a Greek Catholic or a Greek Orthodox. Now tell me, where does your father come from?"

"He comes from Syria, Sister."

She squeezed her cross in the palm of her hand before continuing her interrogation, "And your mother, where's she from?"

"From East Beirut."

She smiled, "And your grandparents, where are they from?"

"From Ghandouriyeh, Sister."

She kissed her cross, mumbling to herself, "Sweet Jesus, a Muslim girl." She took me by the collar of my little white dress, "Come on, follow me, go play in the courtyard with the others. You're not allowed to go to catechism. You're Muslim."

And, thrust into that chasm of which I understood nothing, I clung to her habit, "Please, Sister Marie-Thérèse, I beg you, don't take catechism away from me, I swallow every host all by myself, I know every story by heart, I love mass, don't throw me out."

In her blue gaze I saw a feeling of pity. She stroked my hair and asked me very gently, "Why do you love catechism so much, my child?"

In a rare impulse of truth telling I answered, "Because of the story of the whore, I love stories about whores."

She kissed her cross and murmured, "Lord, they'll never change," then screamed in my face, "Out, out of here!"

I've seldom been subjected to such injustice. I waited for the mass to end. I slipped into the chapel to take my revenge. I climbed on a chair and peed in the font of holy water. Suddenly the door opened. Sister Emmanuelle took me by surprise, with my panties down and my dress raised. She stopped my ears up with Laughing Cow cheese and then locked me up in the cell with the rats, where I spent many hours. Only this time I didn't expect Jesus Christ to arrive.

6 I HAVE NO MEMORY OF THE SKY. WHAT REMAINS in my memory of that year is something dark, like the smoke of burning tires. In just a few days everything fell apart. Actually, the war had been brewing for years, for a century. We very quickly learned to find the safest corners in the apartment and how to put plastic over the windowpanes to avoid their

shattering. When the shooting came too close to the house, my father would get us out of bed and settle us in the vestibule where it was safer. Our grandparents had moved in with us, abandoning their sixth-floor apartment, which was too open. We spent the days listening to the program *Amné wa salké* (How to save your hide), whose presenter provided hour-by-hour information on roadblocks, on checkpoints to avoid, and on safe passages to take. Life was lived by the sound of bullets and always with the voice of Fairouz who made us forget the war. In the summer things quieted down a little, but in September the city suffered very heavy bombings. In the East, the Phalangists were putting up barricades everywhere. They screened people according to their religious denomination, noted on identity cards. Muslims were systematically shot. We couldn't stay in the East any longer, especially because of the persistent rumor that the Phalangists were planning to clean out that whole part of the city. Our parents decided to send us to the South, to Arnoun.

We left Beirut one September morning in my father's blue Volkswagen. He was humming Bedouin songs as my mother was trying to adjust the radio to listen to the news. We heard an enormous explosion as if the heavens were splitting apart above our heads. Beirut's indigo-blue sky suddenly turned black. Through the back window the city looked like a burning mush-room. The radio interrupted its music to announce this bit of news: Israeli fighter planes had just bombed Bei-rut's refinery. Firemen were trying to control the gigan-tic fire. Rana was putting nail polish on her toenails. Nayla was eating pistachios.

A few minutes later another news flash: during the night Palestinian militiamen had taken over the Christ-ian village of Damour and decapitated more than seven hundred people—women, children, and elderly citi-zens—in retaliation for a massacre the Christian Pha-langists had committed in a Palestinian camp.

I asked Nayla for some pistachios. She didn't have any left, so I bit her thigh.

We found shelter with our grandparents in Arnoun and were registered with the nuns in Nabatiyeh. A car would come and get us in the morning and take us home in the afternoon. We forgot about the war. Our parents went back to Beirut after putting a heater in the living room for us because winter was on its way. It was very cold. I remember the day when I opened my eyes and saw nature dressed entirely in white. It had snowed during the night. The Beaufort citadel looked like an iceberg, floating beneath a stark blue sky. There was no one around. The roads were blocked. The driver couldn't come to take us to school. I believe that every beautiful memory of childhood comes from the times that you miss school. I was walking by myself in the middle of the fields when I suddenly saw a dark silhouette emerge, a spot on the snow. It was a small black child, very black. It was the first time in my life that I'd ever seen one. Very curious, I went over to him, "Hello, what's your name?"

He was shivering but smiling, nonetheless, "My name is Shadi."

"And where are you from?"

"From Abidjan."

Good little Lebanese girl that I was, I immediately corrected him, "There's no Abidjan here in the South."

"You fool, Abidjan is in Africa."

Africa I knew, since when I was born my father had been recruited by an uncle, a diamond merchant, to come and make his fortune in Sierra Leone. He stayed for a year. He made a lot of money, blew it in a month, and then came home pockets empty but with a torrid love story he had had with an African woman to whom he was to dedicate an erotic novel.

The little boy was very beautiful. And such a contrast with the snowy landscape. I took him by the hand to show him the citadel. I remember that at one point I felt the irresistible urge to feel his testicles. But when

I saw how he was shivering I felt sorry for him. I don't think he would have survived that little lustful game.

Later I learned that those Lebanese who had emigrated to Africa in droves very often had children with their employees or domestic help but would refuse to leave their progeny behind with those "savages" and sent them "home" instead to their family in Lebanon.

On Christmas Eve, my parents came to take us to Beirut to celebrate. My father was so obsessed with the idea of a party that he didn't even worry about the ever-increasing number of barricades lining the road to the South, where one could disappear at any moment. We were cut off from the world, the car radio no longer worked. We arrived at sunset. The mountain road was crowded with people, wandering vendors were selling coffee and cakes, the Cave of Pigeons was blazing in the setting sun, and there was that cold wind that makes the sky seem higher. All the mountain homes were beginning to be lit up. But a strong smell of blood held sway over the city. My father stopped the car in front of his newspaper office and came out a few minutes later with a long report: the Phalangists had killed two hundred Muslim civilians in revenge for four Christians who'd been found dead in Broumaneh. The person responsible for the massacre, someone not in the least disposed to this kind of crime, was a journalist at the *Orient-Le Jour* who had lost a son early in the war. His oldest son, Roland, had enlisted in the Tigers, the most murderous of all the Phalangist militias. He was found dead on December 5. Armed to the teeth, his father went into Beirut on the sixth and single-handedly executed seventy-five people. I have the testimony in front of me:

" . . . I head for the Shiites who've been spared for the past hour. To liquidate them. All of them. We weren't human anymore. Wolves are undoubtedly less cruel. The Muslims, most of them dockworkers, were killed with a single bullet to the head. With revolvers or Kalashnikovs. We piled up the corpses in a covered truck. Militias transported them and threw them off a bridge. The ones who'd gone most mad were victorious. I didn't feel any satisfaction: I felt no joy, no exaltation. I fired because there was no one innocent anymore, there was no innocence anymore. Every Muslim was responsible for the death of my sons!"

That's when I began to realize that this war was going to transform both executioners and victims into something worse than wolves.

7 WHEN WE RETURNED TO ARNOUN GRAND-
father had a surprise for us. He had painted
the stones of the house's facade in yellow lac-
quer. We spent our winter evenings around the char-
coal stove where we would cook potatoes. Although my
mother was in Beirut, she was with us all the time. We'd
hear her voice on the radio every hour on the hour as
she read the news and the numbers of those who had
been killed.

On Sundays I'd go off with Grandfather to help with
the tobacco picking, which was done exclusively by
women. The entire South was covered with this emer-
ald-green plant that withers in your hand the minute
you pick it.

At the school of Nabatiyeh, the nuns taught us how
to evacuate the classrooms. It was cold but we were
not allowed to close the windows because the Israeli
planes flew over every day, breaking the sound barrier.
The number of families who'd sent their children to the
South so they would be safe was enormous. There were
more than sixty of us in every class. I was overjoyed to
be back in the catechism course.

At recess, we'd hear the most terrible stories about
the Phalangists; it was said that they invaded the town
districts and villages to force all the little girls to sit

down on Coca-Cola bottles. While we were singing "Sous le pont d'Avignon," F-16s were blowing up bridges and roads. There were so many explosions that it made me laugh. I just laughed so I wouldn't be scared.

There was a truce for a few days, which coincided with the Feast of Achourah when Shiites are dressed in mourning for the assassination of the sons of the Imam Ali. I happened to be in the center of town where all the shops were closed. Suddenly I saw thousands of men appear, their heads shaven. Some were whipping their back with chains, others were pounding their heads with the flat side of a sword until blood spurted out. The women, all dressed in white and weeping, were beating themselves brutally. It was very, very hot. The air was filled with the dust of the bombings. The blood that the men shed smelled like rotting flesh. I squatted down to vomit on my sandals.

Our parents kept braving the barricades to be with us whenever they could. Thanks to his press card my father was able to get around. The road to the South was frequently cut off. Each group rigged up its own barrier to rob or murder people, depending on their mood that day. Then you had to pass through the mountain.

My father always arrived with his pockets full of gadgets. He had a weakness for cigarette lighters with naked women and had just discovered those small sake cups that, once they were full, showed a beautiful Asian nude at the bottom. He also had every possible newspaper with him, all of them covering the war and nothing else. He would read them, one after the other, seething all the time, "All of this is the fault of religion; it's that damned God who causes this shit everywhere. When churches and mosques become brothels, that's when we'll have peace."

Throughout the summer of 1976 the war raged on. The Lebanese Left was on the verge of defeating the Phalangists. The battle around the Palestinian camp of Tell el-Zaatar was in the process of turning to their advantage. My father had taken out a fine bottle of arrack. I was dancing on the table with Nayla. Around eight o'clock, Radio Lebanon stopped broadcasting music and played the national anthem. A few minutes later, the Maronite president Sulayman Frangié announced that he was calling on the Syrian army to help save the Christian forces from defeat. My father stood frozen. He was beside himself and his voice was shaking, "Those poor Christians think Damascus is going to save them from the Palestinians; yes, first they'll slaughter the Palestinians and then they'll be back one day and turn against the Christians. That rabble is on nobody's side, they're neither Christians nor Muslims, they're assassins and plunderers who want to rob Lebanon as if it were a bank."

My mother and sisters went to bed while I stayed alone with my father. The air smelled of the tobacco that was growing in the fields. He took out a bottle of arrack and lit his candle, while the radio was softly giving out the news from Tell el-Zaatar. My father was muttering, "I know them, it'll be a bloodbath, it'll be a bloodbath."

I didn't want to go to sleep that night. After three glasses and a pack of cigarettes, he suddenly got up, took a suitcase, and began to pack his things.

"What are you doing, Papa?"

"I have to go, I can't stay here, my girl."

"You're always gone."

"The Syrians are coming, daughter, I can't stay here."

But I didn't understand. I clung to him, wrapped my arms around his legs.

"But you are Syrian, Papa, you can't possibly be afraid of the Syrians."

He burst out laughing.

"Come here, daughter, and let me tell you a story. You weren't born yet when I decided to fight for the liberation of Palestine. I left my teaching position and found myself at the Israeli border, in Chebaa, to get political training from the fighters. A month later I was summoned to attend a meeting in Damascus. Upon my arrival, I was arrested by the Syrian secret service and locked up in the mountain prison. No one knew where I was. They gave me one pound a day with which to feed myself, wash myself, and buy some smokes from our guard. They announced that they were going to shoot me and send my body to my family, covered with the Syrian flag and a note, 'Killed in action for Palestine.' For months I waited in my cell. Every time I heard any steps, I told myself they were coming to get me and shoot me. Months went by. I didn't know how many, I just wanted to see it end. I went on a hunger strike for a week. They set me free without any explanation, the same way they'd arrested me. The cell door opened, the Minister of the Interior himself was there. He was a friend I'd known at the university. He tapped me on the shoulder, and said, 'Hey, there, citizen, how's it going?'

'Fine,' I answered.

'Excuse us, but it was merely a pedagogical experiment,' he said.

'You ought to send all the writers of the Syrian Writers Union here, they'll stop being functionaries and become real authors.'

The minister interrupted me, 'All these months were pointless apparently, you're as sarcastic as ever. And I actually thought they'd reeducate you.'

He took a document with the presidential letter-head from his briefcase. 'On the order of the leadership of the Baath Party, Mr. Assim al-Joundi has been named Director of Moral Counseling.'

It was a nightmare. I flatly refused. He insisted, 'You can't refuse, it's either this or a year under house arrest.'

I opted for house arrest. The day they allowed me to leave the country, I swore I'd never set foot in Syria again. There you have it, my girl, now you know every-thing, now go to sleep."

I woke up at dawn. My father was no longer there.

8 A FEW WEEKS LATER WE HEARD THAT MY father had found refuge in Baghdad. That coun-try not yet in the hands of Saddam Hussein was welcoming every opponent of the Syrian regime with open arms. My mother decided to join him immediately. The Beirut airport had just been closed. She took the boat from Tyr to Alexandria from where she planned to get to Cairo and then take a plane to Baghdad. She'd

embarked on a Cypriot freighter whose captain had taken a Lebanese hooker on board. Crazed with love and alcohol, he ended up losing his way at sea. At dawn, my mother, who was watching for Alexandria from the bridge, saw Israeli vessels appear from all directions and surround the boat to search it from top to bottom. After an entire day of interrogation, the Israelis ended up letting the passengers go. Drunk and in love, the captain hadn't thought of restocking the food supplies. My mother made the crossing to Alexandria on a package of crumbled cookies. It was her first cruise.

In Arnoun life followed the same path as the war. Our evenings were spent around the stove. Grandmother taught me how to prepare grape leaves stuffed with rice, which is how I learned to roll joints so well. Grandfather would recount his exploits with Sharif Hussein's army, still waiting for someone to come knocking on the door one night and ask for the flag of the liberation of Jerusalem. At the same time, the Israelis weren't forgetting about us. Very often the loudspeakers would wake us up in the middle of the night. The Druze auxiliary forces would shout in Arabic: "You have thirty minutes to evacuate the village. The Israeli army has nothing against the Lebanese, it merely wants to liberate you from the Palestinian terrorists." Then we'd flee across the fields in our nightwear, often leaving bits of our sandals and skin behind on the brambles. I began to hear the villagers curse the Palestinians whom they had welcomed as liberators and who were now behaving like an unadulterated occupying force.

Early in the fall of that same year, my mother decided we needed to join our father in Baghdad, but we still had no papers and we had to go through Damascus to get passports. One fine morning Walid, the taxi driver, came to pick us up. The sky was dark with F-16s. The radio was airing the list of the Palestinians whom the Syrian army had killed in Tell el-Zaatar, my grandmother was loading the trunk with every Lebanese dish she could fit in, asking my grandfather every few minutes, "*Ya habibi*, do you think the Iraqis know how to cook?"

Rockets were raining down on the road to Arnoun.

In Damascus, a police officer with a mustache appraised our little girls' legs for a long time before he gave us passes. We took the road to Baghdad that goes through the Syrian Desert. I've never seen such emptiness, such tedium. A landscape bleak as a dried tobacco leaf stretching across hundreds of miles.

What a reunion! My father had rented a ground-floor apartment with a palm tree in the garden, a reminder of his Bedouin childhood in Salamiyeh. He could go on forever about the hundreds of varieties of dates there were in Iraq. We lived not far from the Tigris in the Masbah district where many foreigners resided. At the time, Iraq was at the forefront of Arab nations because of its educational system and its 100 percent literacy rate. The country had trained a true intellectual and scientific elite, with a majority of women in the medical field.

My parents had become good friends with the spokesman of the Palestine Liberation Front, Bassam. He had just survived a Mossad assassination attempt. The package bomb blast had ripped his hands to shreds and completely burned his face, which showed purplish-red scars from the shards. Women shrieked when they saw him, but that first evening when Bassam came to our house I rushed up to him, touched his hands, the skin of which had been burned, and all I could feel was the bare, healed flesh, which was so soft; I looked at his large eyes, so luminous in that face totally destroyed by fire, and said, "I love you."

It was my first declaration of love.

He was married to a very beautiful Lebanese Maronite who was to remain loyal to us forever.

Baghdad was like an immense wind tunnel of hot, sometimes blazing air. The enormous avenues were interspersed with huge water fountains. At night, when the air became breathable again, we would go to the park where statues had been erected in honor of ancient Arab poets: Ibn Zaydûn, Al-Maari, Abû Nuwâs. The gardens overlooked the river and my father would sing of Granada's nostalgia. On the café terraces, Iraqis were drinking one beer after another, lining up the empty bottles on the table. The one who had the longest line of bottles by the end of the evening was the winner.

One night the Lebanese singer Nasri Chams Dine came to our table. Arrack was flowing freely. The lights of the fishing boats hovered on the river and, eventually, the fishermen came to join us and sing along with our star. Grandfather would disappear now and then, returning happier each time. Intrigued, my father finally followed him to find out whether he was secretly guzzling beer.

"Well now, you good Muslim, I thought that your ball-breaker of a God forbade you to drink any alcohol."

Grandfather swore that it was medically prescribed. He suffered from kidney problems and the doctor had told him to have a few beers each day.

"God is merciful and forgiving."

My father had started a free radio broadcast to Syria, inciting the population to rebel against the dictatorship in Damascus. He was convinced that "revolutionary"

Iraq would establish democracy and secularism in the region.

Then he warned us, "My daughters, as long as I'm alive I don't want to see any one of you lift your ass in the air to pray, or to starve yourselves for Ramadan, for that matter."

My mother had found a job at the radio station where she hosted an evening program on poetry. It was the latest thing among the Arab Left; all those who came to the house already saw themselves in Jerusalem. They lived in hotels and everything took place in the lobbies and bars.

In my parents' absence, Bassam taught me how to handle weapons. I knew how to dismantle a Kalashnikov and put it back together again with my eyes closed. I dreamed of hijacking planes later on to better succeed in conquering his heart.

My father had registered us at the Jewish School of Baghdad. It consisted of white Swiss chalets, isolated in a large park. We were the only goys in the school. Sephora, our teacher, made us sing all the time. One April morning the police burst into our classroom, stopped the lesson, and closed the school. Together with my sisters, I was put on a green bus that dropped us in front of a dilapidated building. Female teachers tore our blue smocks off and forced us to put on black dresses. After some patriotic songs, we saw a sheikh come into the room wearing a black robe, carrying the Koran, and waving a stick. Nayla fainted while I got a case of nervous giggles that withstood all the blows of the sheikh's stick. Having been notified, my father managed to let us have piano lessons during the hour that the Koran was taught.

That night, he gave a grand party to celebrate our liberation from religion, where a young man appeared who clearly stood out above the rest. He was always immaculately dressed in a white suit with a white tie and a handsome watch on his wrist. He always brought a bouquet of flowers for "Assim's daughters." We called him "the prince" but he had people call him "Salem." He would bounce me on his knees and taught me to play poker. He was very close to my father, who was to write a book about him.

The Beirut airport had just reopened and we decided to go back, leaving my father behind in Baghdad. Leaving everyone in Baghdad meant the end of an era, the end of childhood. I wrote a long love letter to Bassam to let him know that I would love him every second, every minute, every day, every year of my life. In the plane Rana came to me and said, authoritatively as ever, "Get up and come with me to the lavatory!"

I followed her without protest. In the narrow aisle she grabbed my neck, "Do you know who Salem is?"

Without thinking I said, "He's a prince from *A Thousand and One Nights*."

Rana looked at me pityingly, "Yes, your Aladdin's real name is actually Carlos, Ilyich Ramirez Sánchez. He's not from Baghdad but from Caracas."

9 EVERYTHING HAD CHANGED IN BEIRUT— people's faces, the roads, the buildings, the color of the sky and of the sea. Everyone was armed. At every street corner you'd run into barricades; every party, every faction put up its own, all the Palestinian factions, the Murabitunes, the Arab nationalists. The worst were those of the Syrian army that humiliated the young by beating them at the drop of a hat. Our mother provided us with false papers to protect us.

The war had cleaned out the multifaith areas and people had taken over the free apartments. It was utter chaos. No one spoke of renting any longer but of occupying, squatting. Sometimes the first door needed to be broken down so that places, abandoned by the owners who had gone into mass exile themselves, could be occupied. Day after day Hamra filled up with refugees who were fleeing from the massacres in the Christian areas.

We'd taken an empty apartment on the coastal road not far from the Lebanese Communist Party headquarters and the editorial offices of the left-wing newspapers. In my father's absence there were no parties anymore; the only happy moments came when we went for ice cream at Beirut Airport's Mary Cream, a taste I've been longing for ever since.

But we still had music, the voice of Fairouz that would rock us day and night, and I believe that since then it's been part of me, not just of my memory but of my very skin. I feel it running through my veins every single day. My sister's voice was just like the diva's. One of my mother's friends, a producer, had noticed it and invited her to participate in a television program for children. When my father heard this, he phoned from Baghdad to ask that I, too, be on the set. My mother had bought us absolutely hideous outfits, yellow blouses with puff sleeves and blue skirts. Once on the set, I turned out to be allergic to the synthetic fabric and kept scratching myself as if I had the mange. While Nayla was singing live, I pinched and slapped the children. At the end of the broadcast, the producer was delighted. It gave him the idea for a TV series about the adventures of two sisters, one angelic and the other demonic. I had just turned eight when I signed my first contract to play the devilish role on a weekly basis.

I had a phenomenal memory and my sister was very thorough and studied her texts, learning them by heart. The broadcast took place every Friday and came on just before the eight o'clock news. It was the only children's program on TV and every child in the country watched it.

Television opened several doors for me, first of all at school where the teachers, moved by my role, refrained from giving me the bad grades I deserved. Then, too, the pastry shop La Gondole refused to let me pay for the chocolate éclairs, which were among the best in the world.

During Easter vacation we went back to Baghdad to be with my father, who was feeling very lonely. Saddam's coming to power had emptied the city of its intellectuals in a matter of weeks. I remember that my father came home at noon one Tuesday for his siesta. There was a knock at the door. I opened it, two big guys with their hands in their pockets asked me, "Where is your father?"

In a split second I understood these were Iraqi Secret Service men. I mumbled, "He's sleeping, he's told us not to disturb him."

With one hand one of them lifted me off the floor,

"Go wake him up or else we'll be forced to do it our-selves."

I knocked on his door, "Papa, wake up, they've come to take you to prison."

He always slept with a gun under his pillow and started to reach for it. The men told him calmly, "Mon-sieur Assim, you have three children, the building is surrounded, put away your toy and follow us, we're just going for coffee."

From that day on the phone stopped ringing, no one knocked at our door, the big living room once overflow-ing with people had all of a sudden become deserted. My mother called every high-ranking official who used to visit my father but no one answered her. No sign of life from my father. We didn't know where he was or for how long they would keep him. After a week of inqui-ries we finally heard that the leaders of the Baath had accused him of being entirely too talkative.

After three weeks in prison he was set free, placed under house arrest, and formally prohibited from writ-ing or going anywhere.

Once in Beirut, my mother began to approach the Syrians asking them to authorize his return to Lebanon. I made the rounds with her to every office of the Syrian army.

I saw the officers and soldiers undress her with their gazes, I often climbed on her lap to protect her, and I was kissing her when one of them whispered in her ear, "And, Madame, what will you give me if I authorize your husband to be returned to us?"

The offices smelled of never-washed combat fatigues, floors were frequently covered with blood stains, and chairs were broken. Only the frames around the image of Hafez al-Assad were clean.

After months of effort, the Iraqis allowed my father to meet up with us in Greece for the end-of-the-year holidays. It was snowing in Athens. I was singing in the streets with my sister and he, drunk with joy and wine, was dancing down the city's alleyways. He'd discovered the *sirtaki* and took himself for Zorba the Greek. He'd just finished the first biography of Carlos, who had given him signed photographs "to be sold at a high price to guarantee his daughters' future." Actually, a few days later he sold them to an Arabic magazine for next to nothing.

We took the plane back to Beirut with Papa. It was a night flight but I couldn't sleep a wink because I was so afraid that he would disappear forever.

10

MY FATHER FOUND ANOTHER JOB AT A newspaper and the house began to fill with poets, musicians, and journalists again.

This was the period of small skirmishes when altercations between neighbors would turn into shoot-outs and a settling of scores. People fought over water, gasoline, fruit, bread, or women. Poker games were often interrupted by rockets streaking through the living room, and in the end we hardly paid any attention to them anymore. Every time there was a lull the Syrian forces would fan the flames. Besides Fairouz, I discovered Bob Marley, Led Zeppelin, and Pink Floyd. I began playing in a new series where I had the role of the daughter of a famous poet. The main actor, a local celebrity, would pick me up in his red convertible and we would cross from west to east without a hitch. One evening, when my father saw me crying bitter tears at a scene on television, he asked, "My girl, how can you cry so well on TV?"

"It's not hard, Papa, all I have to do is think of having a father like you and the tears begin to flow all by themselves."

He passed on his passion for books to me, would read to me for hours on end, passages from Dostoyevsky, Baudelaire, Mayakovsky, or the Arab erotic writers. In order to avoid seeing the war we'd explore the galleries, bookshops, or Hamra's movie houses where I saw *Emmanuelle* and *A Clockwork Orange* with him.

Throughout the time that the Israeli occupation lasted we never set foot in Arnoun. When we went back in the summer of 1979, the South had just seceded and was living under the terror of an army financed by Israel. Nothing, not a wall, not a stone was left of Grandfather's house. Utterly bewildered, Grandfather was looking everywhere for his cabinet, his flag, rummaging through the ruins, before he fell down on the remnants of wood and ashes. The Palestinians had occupied the house during the winter and had warmed themselves with the wood of his cabinet and even with the flag of the liberation of Jerusalem.

The region was buzzing with rumors about the atrocities the Palestinians had committed, the rapes, the robberies, and the murders. The people in the South no longer showed the same solidarity with them, worse in fact, they were becoming downright hateful towards their "brothers" of yesterday. In Beirut their reputation smacked of heresy as well. Their leaders, who had a fabulous war chest at their disposal, spent their time going from palace to palace in large black Mercedes-Benzes escorted by bodyguards and prostitutes dressed from head to toe in Christian Dior and Prada.

One afternoon in the middle of July I was on the set. I had a monologue with myself in the mirror when I suddenly felt an awful pain as if my body had been caught in a centrifuge. I never forget my lines, but that day I went blank more than once. My belly was hurting; I wanted to pee. I went to the toilet and lowered my white panties and saw they were covered in blood. My father had told me about the physical changes in young girls, about contraception and periods. I knew all that, but I was scared. I cried. My mother left work in a panic and had alerted my father. Bombs were falling on the road. In the front seat I was crying. The sun was setting over the sea. Smiling, my father was waiting for me in front of the building with a bouquet of flowers and a box of Tampax.

He had explained everything to us about inter-course. His bedroom adjoined ours. The rooms were separated by a large glass window that he had painted indigo blue because he knew we were nosy. He slept with the door open except on the nights they made love. And every time they'd retire together I'd run to spy on them through the keyhole, which he never failed to block with a handkerchief.

I was an inquisitive child, one who looked at the world keenly.

Since my mother was hosting a Lebanese radio

program for the army, we were allowed into the military pool. I was wild and rough, looking for the craziest underwater games. Our days were spent drinking beer, eating pistachios, and staring at boys' bodies.

That's when I felt my first sexual turmoil, touching someone else's skin, feeling the suntan lotion on the back of others, guessing at the size of their sex organ through the wet swimsuit. I was dating a young boy, Sobhi, a love story that consisted of going out to eat French fries at Heinz's, nothing more. I wanted him to caress me, touch me, kiss me, but he was afraid. I talked it over with my father who advised me, "Be careful, daughter, Arab men know nothing about women and if she should make the first move he'll take to his heels."

He'd started to publish *The Memoirs of Carlos* in serialized form in an Arab weekly. The phone rang day and night and he was receiving the most incredible proposals from newspapers that were offering to buy the photos and manuscript from him, but he refused them all. With the rights he held he managed to buy the apartment we were living in without putting it under his name. After three issues were out, he received some very serious threats. He immediately stopped the publication of his story and devoted himself to less disquieting chronicles in which he informed all Beirut about our flirtations, the budding of our breasts, and our periods.

Our exchanges were becoming more and more epic. Having been raised to be entirely free, we didn't understand it at all when he wanted to impose restrictions on us, some of which were outlandish. For example, he had forbidden us to sleep anywhere other than at home.

Nayla, who liked to spend the night at the house of one of her friends, clashed with him when he refused. Sickened by this libertine father who'd turned into a freedom killer, she attempted suicide by swallowing a box of aspirin. Terrified, I wanted to alert my father who came running to the bedroom and, seeing the empty aspirin box, said, "Let her croak if she wants to kill herself over a night at her friend's."

At that moment I hated him with all my heart, hated that strange power he'd assumed out of the blue. I was repulsed by this betrayal from a father who'd always refused any kind of authority and was suddenly becoming authoritative. I wanted to kill him. My older sister agreed with me, it was all just too much.

My sister and I went to the Mazen Pharmacy. At the time Beirut was infested with big rats, so big they made enough noise to equal a cavalry. We asked the pharmacist for something with which to kill "the biggest rat in the city." He handed us a yellow box with a kitschy rodent drawing on it and warned us that it was a very potent poison.

My father's schedule was extremely regular; he left early in the morning for the paper, came home for lunch at noon, and had a siesta before going out again. He was sleeping when we returned. He liked me to make him a cup of Turkish coffee when he woke up, so I heated the water and poured the entire contents of the box of rat poison in it. As he put the cup to his lips he made a face, "This coffee tastes very strange."

I reassured him, "Just drink it, Papa, it's the chlorine and that's good, no bacteria in the water."

He gulped it down. Gloating, I looked at my sister, waiting for him to collapse, struck down forever. But no, he put on his hat, picked up his briefcase, and kissed us before heading for the newspaper. We ran to the balcony to watch him fall down in the street. He walked very straight and with lively step. We waited for an hour to call his office, hoping that his colleagues would tell us he'd died, but alas, it was he on the other end of the line, "Need something, my little angels?"

We hung up. When he came home that evening he merely complained about a bit of diarrhea.

I think that death had become so trivial with the war that we weren't taking any of it seriously anymore. We weren't really thinking of killing our father that day, just of removing the obstacle that kept us from sleeping at our friends' house.

After meeting secretly for two hours, we decided that shooting him with his gun and making it look like suicide would be more effective. We spent a lot of time preparing our version: "He was sleeping in the living room. We made his coffee. He took his gun that was underneath his pillow and put a bullet through his head." While he was sleeping, I took the Smith & Wesson from his briefcase. Not to leave any fingerprints, I had borrowed my mother's fuchsia kitchen gloves. I was tiptoeing around, he was snoring with his mouth open, and as I reached him I saw my hands in that hideous color and their contrast with the gun, which made me burst out in uproarious laughter. We went on the attack several more times but each time the sight of those ghastly gloves made us double up with laughter. We gave up trying to kill our father, telling ourselves that one day we'd take revenge on our mother over those kitchen gloves.

11 KNOWN AS JABARA THE INTREPID, MY grandmother, a tall, very beautiful woman with a steadfast character, fell ill. The disease destroyed her very quickly and she died at the age of fifty-eight. I used to accompany her to che-

motherapy. We were very close. I knew she was going to die and I wanted to spend as much time with her as possible. She had asked to be buried in Arnoun, but the Israeli army that occupied the South turned us away. I still have a profound sense of injustice around that affair: What right does anyone have to forbid someone to be buried in her own land? We interred her in Nabatiyeh, while little girls with head scarves were dancing around her grave to express the joy of seeing her in paradise.

It was at this time that the police of the Baath parties of Syria and Iraq were persecuting the intellectuals and writers who had found refuge in Beirut. We had frequent visits from my uncle Ali al-Joundi, a poet, who was mad, funny, always surrounded by women, drank a lot, and insulted the Syrian president, Hafez al-Assad, in the streets of Damascus. The cops picked him up with a great deal of deference, "The President has ordered us to tell you that if you ever run out of arrack he will have some delivered that same evening."

Something unheard of in Syria's history, Ali had spent his life as a dissident without ever being in prison for a single night.

In January 1980 my father's coworker, a German journalist in Beirut, was found murdered in front of his home with two bullets in his head.

On June 3 that same year my father woke up early, as was his wont. He grabbed his briefcase and put on his hat. He wanted to make sure he had his gun but then remembered that one of his colleagues had reminded him he was a writer and not a militiaman, and so he'd given up carrying a weapon. He took the street that goes up to the paper. When he reached the Mazen Pharmacy he noticed something odd; he saw a yellow Audi parked in the middle of the street. In his memoirs he recounts that he felt nothing other than seeing red and white circles before his eyes, and then everything went black. He swears that the person who shot at him was an acquaintance, which is why he didn't come any closer. The bullet from the silencer smashed the stem of his glasses, which made it swerve toward his upper skull. He fell down in a pool of blood. He says that he saw dozens of young men armed to the teeth surrounding him but no one dared help him for fear that the assassins would react. He stayed there, bathed in his blood, until a Palestinian woman came by who recognized him and began to curse at the motionless crowd, "Do you know who this is? Don't you have any respect anymore to let people just die like this like dogs?" She stopped a car that one of my father's former students happened to be driving who was very willing to take him aboard. But in the interim my father had opened his eyes; he insisted on letting us know, and then began to hit the driver who finally stopped in front of our building. My father got out of the car, took a few steps, and fell into a coma. I heard screaming, rushed to the balcony, and saw him in the middle of a huge red puddle: everything was red, the ground, his body, the street, the city.

I dissolved into tears, and to think that only recently I'd wanted to kill him. All Beirut was at the hospital, including Yasser Arafat and the leaders of the PLO. It took the doctors ten hours to extract the bullet from his brain. I went to see him through the glass window in the recovery room. His head was covered in bandages, his nose and forehead broken from his falls after the attack. His deep blue eyes were swollen. He looked like a fledgling bird barely out of its egg, its protruding eyes covered with fluid. I had the impression that my father had shrunk. He was sleeping all curled up, his hand on his right ear.

Everyone knew that the Syrians were behind the attack but nobody dared to say so. In his memoirs he would later write, "I don't know who wanted to kill me and I don't want to know." At the same time, the assault also seemed like an adventure to me. We were the center of interest in all of West Beirut. I was stuffing myself with *manaïchs* and cheese sandwiches at the hospital cafeteria. I would tell my Uncle Ali dirty jokes and he'd cry, "My niece is a criminal, she laughs at her father's disaster."

My father spent months in a coma. The day that he opened his eyes he asked to play poker. When he came out of the hospital his right side was paralyzed, he could hardly see, and was in a lot of pain, for he had lost part of his cranium. Palestinians stood guard in front of the house to protect him; he came out of the coma totally muddled, confusing names and faces and revealing secrets from some people to others.

My mother carried the whole burden. She wanted to get us away from the house, from our father's deteriorated image. Very often we were followed by men who vanished at first sight.

For the first time in my life I saw my Uncle Khaled, Syria's great union leader. He had spent his life in various prisons and under house arrest. He had asked for special permission to visit his younger brother and I have no idea by what miracle it was granted to him. Uncle Khaled was a large man with a handlebar mustache and emerald green eyes. It was the first and last time I ever saw my father cry, and it was also the last time that the whole Al-Joundi family was reunited. They were so relentlessly persecuted by the Syrian regime that they couldn't even attend each other's funerals.

The doctors had warned us that our father could only be properly taken care of in France. But Grandfather, who had Alzheimer's, was steadily deteriorating. My mother was praying that he wouldn't die in her absence. The day she decided to accompany my father to Paris she said farewell to Grandfather. The moment she closed the door behind her, he breathed his last breath. She postponed the trip so she could attend the funeral.

My parents stayed in Vannes, Bretagne, for months, and my father always had unforgettable memories of the Gulf of Morbihan: "Do you realize, girls, it has 365 islands?"

At last he was going to see Paris where in the sixties his oldest brother had been posted as Ambassador of Syria. Known by every French intellectual, Francophile to the bottom of his soul and in love with Paris, Samy used to tell my father about the cafés, the Latin Quarter, and Montparnasse, and be irate when Papa confused Le Flore and Les Deux Magots. He fell in love with a Jewish woman before writing a book *On Arabs and Jews*. He was called back to Damascus and thrown in prison. General de Gaulle refused to accept his successor's letters of accreditation until my Uncle Samy was released.

Nine months later our parents came back to Beirut, but by then we had become independent, or almost.

12

WHEN HE RETURNED FROM FRANCE my father was no longer able to drive, but he was still macho enough to loathe having my mother at the steering wheel, especially when he was drunk. On these rare occasions when he felt his oriental man's virility wounded he would go into a wild rage, "Who's the man here, anyway, surely not your mother, it's your father."

He'd be staggering but it was impossible to reason with him, and he'd take us home weaving his way and singing and out of pure fear we'd sing along with him.

We had a Volvo we called the T-72 after the Soviet Union's armored cars. It was so old that mushrooms were growing on the floor. We'd get in the backseat taking care not to crush them, and when we got out our father would shout, still staggering, "Well, girls, was it a good crop?"

In Beirut everything was falling apart around us, in the first place the city, but our ideals as well. The Palestinians, who in our eyes were the personification of purity, were descending into violence and debauchery. In the East the militias were better organized, in the Druze Mountain, Joumblatt junior—reigned with an iron hand, but in the West it was utter chaos. Every building lobby had its party, its ideology, and its world vision. However, the left hadn't raised its children to hate other people. My mother, who only rubbed shoulders with Christians, felt that part of her body had been amputated since the communications with the East had been severed. Although she was a Shiite she had never worn the veil, never observed Ramadan, and she smoked and drank. Every time he passed a mosque my father would warn us, "Look, daughters, look how they're down on the ground. You . . . you are never to offer your ass up to the sky. Offer it to men as much as you want, but not to the good Lord. You may drink, go out, lose your virginity, but—let me repeat—in my house I don't ever want to see anyone pray or fast."

In the meantime, he loved the Christian rituals. When he arrived in Lebanon he was teaching at a Catholic school. He would secretly go down into the cellar to steal a few bottles of wine. The priest became aware of it and gave him a talking-to. My father answered him that he had no proof whatsoever and it was just an assumption, "What would you say, Father, if I told people that Marie, the village seamstress, inspires extraordinary erections in you?"

The priest blushed and raised his hands to the heavens, "Oh, no, not that! If you need wine I'll give you as much as you want."

No members of the entire Al-Joundi family ever had religion forced upon them. My Uncle Ali had two daughters who converted to Christianity. At our house the only two sacred objects were an olive-wood statuette of Guevara and an icon of the Virgin given to my father by a Soviet Communist Party member. That education was what saved us. In the West we lived in a small republic that brought Christians and Muslims together, the majority of which was struggling to have Lebanon recognize an eighteenth community, that of the atheists.

I was doing publicity for General Electric, Arthur Martin fridges, Brandt dishwashers, and Calor irons. The sound of the war was there at all times, interrupting our lives. I used to go to the movies by myself at the Concorde in Verdun. I remember *Endless Love*. I cried my eyes out over Lionel Richie and Diana Ross's song. I learned English by bellowing Chris de Burgh's "Traveller." I danced like Travolta. I'd go to Uncle Sam's in Rue Bliss where the young men were hanging out at the bar with their whiskey, white towels knotted around their neck, waiting for the barber to come by and clip their beards. I spent a lot of time at the theaters, whose big names, Roger Assaf and Raymond Jbara, had stayed in Beirut. Ziad Rahbani, Fairouz's son, staged plays that made fun of our revolutionaries and made us laugh at the war. I loved watching Dina Haydar dance, beautiful beyond belief and firing up the Baalbek nights.

The city had become a wasteland. Since there were no public services anymore, each district had arranged to rent its own pickup trucks to collect the garbage, which was then dumped outside of town where the poor refugees from the South were living. Their children played on mountains of trash to the never-ending sound of gunfire. Since the war began, we'd been living by gaslight and generators. Their noise enveloped Beirut day and night while they emitted an acrid oily smoke. It was easy to recognize from afar and by the noise whether a generator was providing light for a rich or a poor home. We dreaded the gasoline shortage that threatened daily, for without gas we had no bread. The city walls were completely covered with graffiti, of which I remember one in particular: "No to religion but yes to Islam."

On the eve of the 1981 summer vacation, the Israeli air force bombed a building where Palestinians were living. The blast of the explosion shattered our classroom windows. We had all fled before that happened except for Nayla who, stunned by the spectacle, couldn't move from her seat. It badly cut her hands and legs.

When he came out of the hospital my father called all three of us together:

"My daughters, I know you're at the age where everything is a temptation and the first of these are cigarettes. I've always told you that in our family it's forbidden to forbid. Since I don't want to see you smoking in secret, here is a cigarette for each of you. You'll smoke in front of me and you'll see how filthy and horrible it is, and then you'll give it up all by yourselves."

The three of us were lined up on the living room sofa. We dragged on our Gauloises without filters and then called out in chorus, "Papa, it's marvelous."

He was livid. None of us has ever stopped smoking since that day. A week later I discovered pot and smoked my first joint, which made me laugh so hard that I saw the sea as much wider and the bullets as less lethal.

13 WHEN I FELT MY BREASTS WERE BEGINning to grow I was very proud and my father applauded heartily. I had a very lean boy's body and was glad not to have any thighs or ass. According to my father, the wider a woman's ass, the more beautiful she is. Not in my case. I'd been waiting for years for the day that I could wear a bra. One July morning I spent an hour in the bathroom looking at myself stark naked. For quite a while I was handling my breasts, which amply filled my hands. I put on a white

shirt and pants. My father was reading his paper and I interrupted him, "Papa, get up."

"To do what, my girl?"

"It's time to buy me a bra."

He almost choked on the smoke of his cigarette.

"You're crazy, a bra? Why not a leash? A bra, do you realize the bondage that suggests? You'll have a corset that will keep you from breathing, the straps will leave marks on your shoulders; do you know how many women I ran away from at the moment of lovemaking just because of that hideous scar, and then the imprint of the hooks on your back look just like bullet holes. No, you'll never wear a bra. Just ask your mother."

"Who buys the bras for my sisters?"

He knew then that he'd lost. On the way, we saw a young man suddenly emerge from an apartment building, rush over to a young girl, put a bullet in her head, and then put a bullet in his own mouth. Both were dead instantly. We were speechless. A neighbor stepped over the bodies as if they were abandoned packages. My father asked her, "What happened to him?"

Unflustered, the woman answered, "A great misfortune, Sir. That was his fiancée, he found out she was cheating on him."

We were at the Saint-Elie Souk in a shop with fine

lingerie run by a woman. My father provided her with all the details of my private life and also insisted on getting information on every cup size. After an hour of conversation I came out with a white Triumph, 32A. At last I was a woman! Mad with joy I was determined to sleep in it. In the middle of the night I woke up on the verge of asphyxiation, I couldn't breathe anymore, tore myself from the bed, took off the bra, and threw it out the window. Since that day I've never worn a bra again.

My father didn't sleep. He stayed up very late, writing, smoking until dawn every night, and listening to Gypsy music. He heard me and knocked on the door, "Are you all right, my girl?"

"Yes, Papa, but you were right, that thing strangles you."

"Good night, daughter. I don't know if they'll ever liberate Jerusalem but at least your breasts have been liberated for good."

The next day I woke up early and was making coffee when I heard an enormous explosion and a split second later every window in the house was shattered. The Israeli air force had just bombed the Cité Olympique. Radio Monte Carlo was shouting:

"In Lebanon the Israeli army is bombing PLO camps in retaliation for the attack on the Israeli ambassador in London. According to the Israeli government, this operation, which has mobilized hundreds of thousands of soldiers, is aimed at cleaning out the entire Palestinian population of Lebanon."

On June 6, 1982, the Israeli army marched on Beirut. The Syrians were the first to take off, passing beneath our windows with their armored vehicles, their turrets laden with everything they'd been able to steal: chandeliers, bathroom sinks, rugs, chairs, sofas, and even bidets. My father was yelling from the balcony, "Murderers, toilet thieves, go home, and wake up!"

Saïda and Tyr fell without putting up a fight. We were all surprised, shocked even, at the disarray. There were actually some Muslim villages that welcomed the Israeli soldiers as liberators. Hamra emptied out in one day and all store shutters were lowered. Our apartment was close to the offices of all the Palestinian organizations and we found shelter at the house of an aunt in Verdun. The F-16s dropped pamphlets in Arabic summoning all the inhabitants to leave West Beirut within seventy-two hours. Nobody expected the city to be blockaded. Since the attack my father no longer worked, as there wasn't a single Lebanese newspaper willing to employ a journalist who'd been condemned to death by Damascus. My mother went to work as if the war had never happened. When my Uncle Samy, who had been living in Hamra for years, went out to buy the paper, he returned to find his building gone. Thanks to his son, an officer in the Syrian army, he was given permission to settle in Salamiyeh where he would end his days under house arrest.

From the balcony of our safe haven in Verdun, I saw the warships clogging up the harbor, bombing us; it seemed as if fire was belching from the sea with every shot. I saw the F-16s launch flares over the coastal road at night, resembling huge orange chandeliers, quivering for a moment before they disappeared in a cascade of stars. I would sing Fairouz to them, "I'm staying with you, alone in the night."

The Israeli army had surrounded West Beirut. Their ships filled the sea, their military vehicles the mountain, and their planes the sky. They cut off the water, the electricity, and prohibited any food and fuel supplies from being brought into the city. Confronted with such a merciless machine of destruction we had nothing.

I wanted to take up arms but my father refused, "It's stupid to die for nothing. You'd be better off putting a bullet through your head, it's easier."

The bombings kept growing in intensity, sometimes going on for nights on end. With each alert my father had us go downstairs to the shelter where it really stank from the humidity. People came down there by the hundreds. I caught scarlet fever as did my sisters, and had many bloody noses. We were starving and dying of thirst. That's when our parents decided to let us go over to the East.

My aunt's husband, who was Christian, was supposed to meet us at the museum passageway. My mother was driving. My skin was ashen, and my hair was sticky with dust and sweat. My body smelled of the bombings, a very strong chemical odor. The uncle was waiting for us on the other side of the demarcation line. The Israeli soldiers stopped us. It was the first time in my life I saw any Israeli soldiers.

My uncle was waiting for us in a brown sedan. We were in the back, terrified of the Israelis. When the Israeli army stopped us again a few meters down the road they asked us to get out of the car, which we did with our arms raised, convinced this was our final hour. I kissed Nayla farewell. It was nighttime and the city was burning behind us. The soldiers were shouting in Hebrew. Their officer came toward us, gave each of us a candy, and wished us good night.

My uncle, who was very pro-Israel, had noticed how deathly afraid we were and to cure us of our "aversion" he confined us to the living room to watch *Holocaust*.

"You don't like the Israelis, now you'll see what they've been through."

No matter how many times we repeated that our

father had taught us that all people were the same, that we felt no hate for the Jews, but that we couldn't accept a foreign army dropping bombs on us for a month. He made us watch Meryl Streep for four hours, rigid and with only one question in our mind: It's true that they have suffered, but why do they have to make us suffer, too?

The next day our uncle invited us to Jounieh, the Saint-Tropez in the Christian zone. The beach was full of synthetic-blond girls with large gold crosses around their necks, kissing dust-covered Sephardic soldiers full on the mouth. The bars were playing loud disco music but it couldn't overpower the bombings. There was champagne on every table and many customers raised their glasses to passing Israeli soldiers to thank them for ridding the country of "the Palestinian vermin."

That evening our uncle insisted on giving a big party in our honor on the terrace of his apartment building in Hazmieh, which overlooked all of Beirut. There was a belly dancer, there were guests dressed in Pierre Cardin, and there was a buffet with salmon, tarama, and piles of pastries and fruit. In the two weeks of the blockade we'd eaten nothing but rotten tomatoes and onions. The belly dancer was calling to the Israeli attack crafts as they bombed Hamra, "Louder, my brothers, louder with that bombing music, louder, make us dance to it."

A group of old ladies, glasses in hand, screamed and applauded at every explosion, "Bravo, kill them all, don't let a single one of them survive!"

Scratching and biting, my sisters and I threw ourselves at them, whereupon my uncle called my mother and begged her to come and get us. "Come and pick up your daughters, they're terrorists, if they stay here they'll risk having their throat cut."

My mother came at dawn to pick us up at the museum passageway. We were stopped at the checkpoint by the Phalangists. The militia frisked my sisters who were hiding apples in their blouses. They confiscated the fruit and sniggered, "Arabs don't eat Golden Delicious, young ladies."

14 WE WENT BACK TO OUR BASEMENT shelter in Verdun. The bombings became more intense and the floor was shaking under our feet. I spent forty-eight hours crouched, huddled in the dark, a deluge of fire and phosphorus outside. I slept with a roll of bread and a *Kiri* under my pillow. Nayla very stylishly wore pumps and was putting on lipstick in the dark, wondering who this army of madmen was that kept an entire population

from taking a shower. In July 1982, after four weeks of blockade, there was nothing left anymore, no water, no bread, no cheese. The Israeli army had cordoned off the city, closed every exit, as in a checkmate. The besieged Palestinians tried to resist but the battle was much too uneven.

Radio Monte Carlo announced that the American envoys had obtained a truce from Israel so the wounded civilians could be evacuated. We came out of our shelter. With the heat, the dead bodies, the bombs, and the trash, Beirut smelled like a rotting carcass. We saw that all the buildings were gutted, the alleys strewn with cooking stoves and refrigerators hurled out by the blast of the explosions. An unspeakable silence reigned in the deserted streets. The sun was blazing hot and the sea still swarming with gray and green battleships. A few birds were singing; in the distance I heard the barking of dogs that now ran around in packs, human thighbones between their teeth. I followed my sisters and at the end of an alley we saw a bombed-out old house with a big garden and a large pond of stagnant water. All three of us jumped in, to drink, to wash. We were naked and green, splashing about among the frogs, our hair covered with algae, but happy as larks beneath the sky of Beirut. It was the most wonderful bath of my life.

My father decided we should leave the apartment

in Verdun, which had been hit; the whole area near the coastal road was in danger of being razed. We went to Wat Wat where, according to my mother, the alleyways are so narrow that no bullets can get through. It was a dark apartment that had been abandoned for years, where the sun never entered. The chairs were broken and the mattresses vomited up their springs. Still, it was only a few meters from the radio station. Finally my mother was able to walk to work and her nearness was reassuring to us. Alone at the wheel, she had crossed the city so many times to make sure the program would be broadcast.

My sisters and I were adamant about doing something, but my father flatly refused to let us take up arms, "Taking up arms is out of the question for my daughters. Arms are for the military, and the military are all fascists."

"But we want to do something to help the people."

"In that case I suggest you go to the Red Cross, they need help."

We immediately joined the Red Cross. After a few hours' training we were admitted as nurses. The team had only one ambulance that couldn't be used because there was no gasoline available. Our first trip dealt with the Concorde movie theater, which had been transformed into a shelter for four hundred families. The wounded were lying on the floor, children burned by fragmentation bombs. People rushed over to hug us, thinking we were there to rescue them, but we had neither serum, nor drugs, nor an ambulance. Helplessly, I simply wept as I watched children die in the seats of the movie house.

The vise around the Palestinians tightened ever more as the Israelis blew up each building to which the head of the PLO would retreat. Since our famous bath we hadn't taken a shower. Buying water was extremely expensive. To clean up we'd pass a lightly moistened washcloth over our faces, while hair washing was out of the question. All we had left to eat was rice, wheat, and lentils; forget fruit and vegetables. My father's friends would come in the evening, each bringing his own treasure of the day: a cucumber, a tomato, a bit of bread, a handful of olives. It was pure luxury!

One night that month my father found a watermelon riddled with shards of glass in a bombed-out house. He came home happy and we wanted to devour it by ourselves, but he insisted that the whole building join the party. So we cut it in tiny cubes and shared it with ten floors of neighbors.

For my father it was a very difficult period; he was no longer working, my mother was at the station all day, and we were at the Red Cross. He couldn't write nor did he have the strength to take up arms. He suffered from terrible migraines and would rub his back against the wall to lessen the pain.

Hamra was deserted, not a single building was standing, the phosphorus bombs burned everything, but at the same time the city was ours. We were alone in the street; we were the queens of the town that belonged to us alone. At last we were all equal. We were all hungry, thirsty, and very dirty. Not a living soul anywhere. I felt I could count on any neighbor or passerby; we were finally worthy of being alive. Besides the noise of the bombs, the district occasionally shook with the cries of soccer fans. It was during the final few days of the World Cup and all Lebanon was riveted to the TV. So that everyone could follow the matches as the bombings continued, and in spite of the blockade, people were putting little TV sets in the street powered by car batteries. We'd sit around in a circle and applaud our special team. I hated Italy when it beat Brazil, my favorite team.

On the radio my mother's voice announced that Arafat had recognized the state of Israel. My father was holding his head between his hands and I, the kid by his feet, was trying to understand: Why all these wars, all these dead, just for this?

For two weeks from August 1, 1982 on, the Israeli air force, navy, and armored cars set fire to Beirut day and night without letting up. We were in a shelter, once again in the dark without water or food, and to quench my thirst I sucked first my skin and then my sister's. On August 20 the United States obtained a cease-fire. Fifteen thousand PLO fighters would be evacuated by the fleets of Western nations.

My father was to write in his memoirs that the most tragic moments of this war were not the images of the Palestinians leaving Beirut, but those of the horses of the city's hippodrome, which had never stopped its races during the civil war but had to suspend them because of the Israeli blockade. Left to their own devices, the horses were roaming the city with the rats and dogs, and sometimes when they stepped on a fragmentation bomb they were blown up. It was a mass grave of horses. We were at the Red Cross. We were going up and down the city. The Palestinians were saying their goodbyes. They fired into the air, but people were on the balconies, and bullets fell back down on the shoulders of those who were waving at them. I spent days extracting bullets from people's shoulders and arms, taking them out with tweezers. My hands had never held so many bullets.

15

WITH THE PALESTINIANS GONE, ISRAEL lifted the blockade. We had plenty of water and the stores opened their doors once again. To celebrate this return to normal life, I decided to eat kebabs for the first time in my life, and when they made me very sick my father sat by my bedside trying to make me laugh, "You've survived the phosphorus bombs, you're not going to die because of one *kefta*."

The TV in the living room was on all day long. The presidential elections were supposed to take place in the fall but no one believed that the Parliament would be able to come together. My whole family was following the procedures live. The bailiff announced the result of the vote count in a very solemn voice, "Gemayel, Gemayel, Gemayel."

The deputies stood up to applaud the new president of Lebanon: Bashir Gemayel. We looked at each other, stunned. We knew the crimes he had committed against his own people, against the Palestinians, and we also knew how friendly he was with Israel. He called Menachem Begin "Papa."

In West Beirut you could hear a pin drop, but in the East there were salvos of joy and champagne was flowing in abundance.

Bashir was sworn in on August 23; on September 14 Israeli troops entered Beirut, violating the cease-fire agreement. The next morning we awoke only to see all the garbage cans and containers full of all kinds of weapons, Kalashnikovs, Uzis, RPGs, pistols, and grenades. People had gotten rid of their weapons during the night because the Israeli soldiers were combing the city. My father put on his suit and tie, expecting them to come for him and arrest him. He wanted to have a last one for the road with me. Things were moving so fast that I didn't even have time to feel sadness or joy. "To your health," I said when we heard shouting in the stairwell. Our fifth-floor neighbor was dragging his only son out by the neck and, in front of the Israeli patrol, put a bullet through his head. Rafiq was sixteen. He had betrayed a Palestinian activist for fifty dollars.

A few days later on the radio, my mother's light-hearted voice announced, "President Bashir Gemayel died this morning in a bomb explosion, set off in the premises of the Phalangists in Achrafieh."

In the West there were salvos of joy and we drank arrack. Many of our Christian friends were relieved, as the man was a danger to every community.

The day after Gemayel's death the Red Cross woke us very early. We had to rush to a field in the southern suburbs. Long before I reached Sabra I could smell an unbearable odor, the same one dogs emit when they've gorged themselves on corpses. It was very hot, but I still wore a mask. The first image I had of Sabra was that of a Palestinian woman, dragging the body of her husband, whose throat had been cut, and screaming at the journalists, "Stop filming us, have you no shame to come here now, you sons of bitches!"

Alleys and homes strewn with bodies of children, women, and old people, all of them distended from the heat. Women were tearing their hair out, shrieking, recounting the night of slaughter in a rush of bits and pieces—the Israeli flares, the arrival of drunken and drugged Phalangists, their pleasure in cutting men to pieces and sticking those up on a wall, raping young girls under the eyes of their families. I saw one murdered family whose eight members were tied to one another by barbed wire, the steel wire buried in their black-and-blue flesh. People recognized their loved ones by their clothes only, they were too disfigured. I held women up as they identified the dead, and I wept and vomited. It went beyond rage, grief, and even madness. I felt as if my own throat had been cut. What frightened me most in Sabra weren't the dead but what could be read on the faces of the living. I had just turned fourteen.

Amin Gemayel succeeded his brother as president. Barely in office, he ordered a curfew for West Beirut.

One could not be outside between the hours of six in the evening and six in the morning. He called for an international force to protect "civilians from any atrocities." Within a few hours the streets of Beirut looked like a military parade with uniforms from every corner of the planet. We felt trampled and invaded by all these foreign armies. I saw myself as very small, as if I were shrinking more and more each day. The new government had passed a law that limited visitors' permits for foreigners to nine months. Like my father and my sisters, a foreigner in my own land, I had the feeling that the Lebanese wanted us to pay the price for my father's Syrian origins, although the Syrians wanted him dead.

In September I went back to school at Carmel Saint-Joseph's, run by left-wing nuns and attended by the children of Lebanese Communist Party leaders. In the cafeteria we listened to Jean Ferrat's "Camarade" and Léo Ferré's "La Solitude" through the loudspeakers. My girlfriends spent most of their time in the bathroom whose windows overlooked the French military base. The majority of them had a lover in the UNIFIL. But my sister and I didn't participate in this game, for our father had warned us, "If you must, make love with a dog but never with a soldier."

In class, I used to drink cocktails of Tabasco and vodka just to annoy the geography teacher who wanted us to memorize the names of all the rivers in France.

In the streets of Hamra I began to run across the first bearded men who spat when they passed an unveiled woman. In the South, Hezbollah —born on the rubble of the Israeli invasion—began to gain power and organize for the defense of this region that for so many years had been completely handed over to misery and occupation.

Since the Israeli invasion I had stopped doing the TV series. The program had changed. The broadcast was altered. I was at an ungrateful age, neither woman nor child, but prematurely adult as well because of the war, which had robbed us of our childhood. Nayla had stopped singing and started playing the lute, while Rana had chosen the guitar and I wanted to play violin. I spent hours tormenting the bow without managing to get the slightest sound out of it, so I decided to put an end to my musical career. After the Palestinians who had occasionally assigned him some freelance work left, my father had no resources at all anymore. Then my mother, who at the risk of her life had kept going, lost her radio programs as well. At that point I witnessed the escalating hatred between Christians and Muslims and several times a day my father would hammer into us, "Without the Christians Lebanon is dead."

The Phalangists were fanning out all over West Beirut, considering Israel's victory over the PLO their own. They were in conquered territory. They would go into people's homes day and night, arbitrarily kidnapping or liquidating the young. The war was taking a different turn. Party time was over.

I felt no real love for anyone whatsoever. I was looking for an impossible love. My father had told me the myth of Plato's androgynous circle: "At first, man and woman were one until the day when the original circle was split in two. Everyone on this earth is looking for the half from which he was cut off." I would look every boy in the eyes and wonder: Is this my half? But I never felt the call of those origins in anyone at all. It wasn't easy to fall in love because the first thing to keep in mind was proximity. Beirut had been so fragmented, broken into infinite numbers of little islands and universes, that it was in a girl's best interest to have a lover on the same street, and preferably in the same building, otherwise her love would be impossible. Since I had no boyfriend of my own, I hung around with ruffians, and when school let out I'd find the adolescents gathered outside the building, talking about motorcycles, music, love, but never about the war, politics, or religion. It was as if they were trying to forget all about the war.

I wore pants. I thought I was unattractive. I bought my clothes at If's and my shoes at a shop run by an Armenian not far from the American university. The store was filled with shoeboxes; he was a little old man with glasses on the tip of his nose, had a small table with a sewing machine and made shoes to size for the whole family. Sometimes I'd go as far as Clemenceau to Le Piaf which made Parisian designer clothes. I'd go shopping with my father who still had the Volvo. Twice it had been knocked over by a bus and the roof was riddled with bullet holes, so that when it rained we were soaked to the skin.

At Carmel Saint-Joseph I discovered the film club where I saw *Hiroshima mon amour*, which helped me look differently at war. I saw all the Arab films made since 1920, as well as the American classics, and kept index cards with notes on every film.

I knew I was going into the theater and nothing else. I read Anouilh, Beckett, and Ionesco, and dreamed of going to the Royal Theatre in London.

In the fall of 1982, the market had smaller generators available and everyone rushed to get them. The nights became intolerable. Beirut echoed like an immense jackhammer around the clock.

Because I spent so much time at the film club, which

was in the basement and reached by a slippery stone staircase, I ended up breaking my leg. One evening after seeing Charlie Chaplin's *The Great Dictator*, I found myself in the middle of a fight between the national movement and the Lebanese forces. I was there with all the girls of my class. The shells were falling behind us. I was on crutches, the fire was coming closer, and at a given moment I felt myself flying above the street. I was running ahead of everyone, straight to the apartment in Verdun and struggled up the ten flights. When I arrived my armpits were bloody. My father caught up with us very quickly. Since the attack he'd become more wary, more considerate, spent hours by the phone, hitting it in the hope that the dial tone would come back. My girlfriends and I felt we were safe. We had taken out the Monopoly set when another shell came straight through the living room. The blast threw me against the wall and we ran for cover in the shelter.

It was raining; the foam-rubber mattresses were soaked through with water and it was very cold. That night all we had were some olives and a cucumber. My father carried me in his arms to the bathroom, which was a hole in the ground. I took my pants off and saw two openings in the left wall through each of which a pair of wide-open black eyes was glimmering. I screamed. My father ran and surprised two Syrian informers in front of the bathroom wall who were observing me while I was peeing. For three days in that winter of 1983 neither the rain nor the fighting ever let up. On the fourth night, my mother, seeing us on the verge of death, took things into her own hands, "If you stay here you'll die. Come, it seems they've just opened a fantastic nightclub on Saint-Simeon Beach."

Beirut was deserted. Before we arrived in Summerland, we had crossed camps where refugees from the South were crowded together in utter misery. Little colored trains, like a Walt Disney movie, picked up the clientele and dropped them off in front of the covered swimming pool where the water came cascading down from a height of ten meters, with a circular bar behind the waterfall. Patrons in tuxedos and evening gowns were sipping cocktails. Young girls clad in T-shirts were diving into the water. From the platform the host was calling to start the most-beautiful-bikini-in-Beirut contest. One kilometer away bombs were raining down on Hamra. I was shivering, I was in my jeans and smelled of mud and mold. I closed my eyes and dove in, too. "It's Raining Men" came from the sound system on this crazy night in Beirut.

16

MY OLDEST SISTER WAS IN LOVE WITH a religious Muslim student. In her passion she imitated everything he did and began to say her prayers and observe Ramadan. She'd lock herself in the bedroom to pray and my father couldn't understand it. I wanted to mimic her, be like her. For me, observing Ramadan was the supreme offense, the unsurpassable rebellion. I started on the first day. A few minutes after the prayer that marked the end of the day's fast, my father called to offer me a glass of whiskey, which I politely declined.

"No, Papa, I have a stomachache."

"Exactly, the whiskey will soothe the pain."

"No, I really want to go see the woman next door."

He became more and more persistent until I ended up by exploding, "No, I don't want your whiskey, I'm observing Ramadan." His large blue eyes filled with tears. He was looking at me, the glass shaking in his hand, and I just stood there determined to go as far as I could. I sensed that I now embodied the failure of all his dreams of freedom, of the secular life. He bellowed, "You're not allowed to observe Ramadan, I forbid it."

He was choking and I retorted, "You have to respect my convictions, that's what you taught me."

He came rushing at me, grabbed me with one hand, and with the other forced me to drink the whiskey. He shouted, "Convictions, my ass, come on, drink, I'm telling you."

I drank. I felt the liquor warming my belly, and I relaxed. "You're right, Papa, it's totally stupid. I'll never do it again."

He kissed my forehead.

One glass of Johnnie Walker Black was the incentive for my first and last spiritual crisis.

The war grew ever more ruthless. Under a pseudonym my father kept a running account, but his paper was receiving daily threats. Our Palestinian friends who'd found asylum in Cyprus insisted that he leave Beirut and join them. He decided to go but the airport was closed and taking the boat from Jounieh, the stronghold of the Phalangists, was out of the question. While waiting for him to depart, I threw myself into becoming a political activist. Each party, each little group had its own radio: the Mourabides, the Phalangists, the Shiite Party, the Communist Party were all organizing training sessions for the young. I was immersed in meetings to explain Marxism to the middle-class youth of my generation, while Carmel gave us permission to participate in demonstrations in support of the national resistance. I thought I was accomplishing an extraordinary feat, being an actress on my own soil and not just following my father. At last I was discovering politics beyond the perimeters of the war and reading Marx and the Bolivian notebooks of Guevara. I was running Communist youth cell meetings in basements and dark rooms.

Early in 1984, the clashes were so violent that we all spent the night in the apartment. My oldest sister was deep into her religion, and Nayla had decided to give up television in favor of the movies. My uncle, a filmmaker, had advised her to go to Brussels.

One night, one of our friends came to tell us that a ship would be waiting for us at dawn and that we had to use one of the small boats on the coastal road to meet him. I had made up my mind not to let my father leave all by himself. We woke up at the crack of dawn as the bean and seed vendors passed by. Having been alerted, the militia began to fire at us but we had some good rowers who moved us quickly beyond their reach. We went on board. The sea was calm and the sky was blue. In the mist I watched Beirut vanish in the distance. We went to the bridge. I saw smoke rising from the various districts as the city gradually moved further and further away; I was weeping with joy because I'd escaped from the shooting, and I wept with sorrow, too.

They were waiting for us in Larnaka and then we went to Nicosia where all the Palestinians who'd been ousted from Beirut, as well as the Syrian opponents, were. We were taken in by a friend with a large, modestly furnished apartment. At that point we suffered from terrible insomnia that no alcohol or tranquilizer could relieve. After the first few days we realized that it was because of the silence that reigned over Nicosia that we couldn't sleep. We recognized the damage the war had done to us. Every time I heard the siren of an ambulance I fled under a table, while my father avoided all the windows whenever he entered anywhere. We learned that life is not war, for as the bombs were falling in Beirut we were told continuously, "This is normal life."

Moved by our plight, one of my father's friends, an official at the Syrian Consulate in Nicosia, had Syrian passports made for us. At last I was able to travel without a pass.

A month later, my father took a plane to Tunis and I went back to Beirut. I found the gang of bikers again, all of them now wearing their hair long. I spent every night at Back Street, a nightclub in the Makhoul just below Hamra. Most of my contemporaries had gone to live abroad, while those who'd stayed were dropping like flies. One night, as I was leaving André's bistro, I saw a young man insult a pedestrian who was standing in the middle of the street. The latter pulled a gun from his pocket, ordered the young man to get out of the car, get on his knees, and apologize. He refused. The other put a bullet between his eyes and then went on his way.

I met Maher, a twenty-year-old homosexual, who wanted to study medicine in the United States. He had blond hair and lived in a minuscule room with a pink ceiling, pink walls, and a pink floor. I'd just turned sixteen and often discussed sex with him. He told me what Lebanese men said about women, how they bragged about popping their hymen like the cork on a bottle of champagne. They didn't say deflowering but breaking, taking the top off, and whenever a man "opens" a girl she is his for life. It made me think of branding cattle as I'd seen it done in American films, which I found appalling.

Maher reassured me, "Listen, you just have to do it yourself."

"That's hard, Maher."

"It's nothing, it's thinner than cigarette paper."

"And I thought it was a chunk of flesh like a steak."

Maher was an encyclopedia. He knew everything there was to know about men and women. I got my education from him. I spent entire days in his room watching porno movies while he'd comment on the advantages of each position. He told me that fellatio is what men prefer. He initiated me by having me practice on a cucumber as he elaborated, "You need to understand that fellatio is an art, just like singing, painting, or fine cooking. First you gently take the penis and hold it firmly in your hand, the tongue should just barely stroke the testicles, with little taps, then slowly move up the penis, licking it like an ice cream cone, then take the glans and put your tongue around it, and only after this long prelude, where nothing is forced and everything's done with the tip of your tongue and your lips, can you take the whole member into your mouth. Don't be afraid of the ejaculation, sperm isn't harmful! It contains two kinds of vitamins, C and B_{12}, but a lot of minerals, too, such as calcium, magnesium, phosphorus, potassium, and zinc. It also has two kinds of sugar: fructose and sorbitol. Remember that sperm is rich in protein, sodium, and cholesterol, and you should know that the average ejaculation has between fifteen and thirty calories. Should you happen to swallow it you're only getting a few extra calories."

I didn't let him finish his explanation. I was in love with Ara, a green-eyed Armenian, and knew that he spent his days at the military swimming pool. I grabbed a cab. And, indeed, he was at the beach. I took him by the hand and walked him to a cabana. Without a word

I pulled down his trunks, took his penis in my mouth, thinking of Maher's words like a cookbook recipe. When I felt the sperm in my mouth I didn't have the courage to swallow it, for Maher had warned me that no Lebanese woman is liberated enough to do that, so I spat it out and saw Ara, collapsed, his mouth open, his pupils dilated, his arms crossed, muttering, "Lord, how beautiful! Thank you, Lord, for this offering."

I'd felt nothing—it was a performance, a purely technical skill, a piece of work well crafted.

The news quickly spread through the group and all the girls at the pool came to see me so I could initiate them. Since my parents were in Tunis, I began to give my first sexual catechism classes to my friends at Carmel Saint-Joseph for five dollars per hour. They would sit in a circle in the living room and, like a priestess, I'd repeat Maher's lesson word for word, cucumber in hand, "Remember, ladies, that fellatio is an art, just like singing, painting, or fine cooking . . . "

17 AT MAHER'S PLACE I TRIED COCAINE. It was June 1984. He put a mirror under a lampshade, took a razor blade to make thick lines with the powder, and handed me a straw.

"Now, keep one nostril closed and inhale through the other. There's an immediate high, it's Bolivian pink known as fish scales."

I snorted the first line, felt as if a grenade had exploded inside my head, as if a thousand projectors were lit in my brain. It was two o'clock in the morning; drunken militiamen were cleaning their weapons and listening to Pink Floyd. I was walking in the middle of the road feeling strangely invulnerable. I was outrageously made-up, my nails were two inches long, and I felt I was in Clint Eastwood's skin, directed by Sergio Leone. I had five grams of coke on me and thought I would be able to slaughter a whole army of Phalangists with that.

I ended my night by emptying a Stolichnaya bottle, stranded somewhere with walls plastered with photos of Marx, Engels, and Lenin, or perhaps at Abou Ali's place, next to the lighthouse. There was a shack where a fisherman had planted a field of cannabis. At daybreak his wife served me grilled sardines.

Not a week went by that I didn't go to the morgue to identify the body of a friend, an uncle, or a cousin. The hospital had become the place to meet everyone. It had replaced the village square.

My visits to the morgue made me furiously eager to make love. One evening I made the acquaintance of

Ramy, a nurse. He suggested taking me home by ambulance. His colleague was driving like mad, and we were on the stretcher, glued to each other. He was kissing me passionately. My tongue was in his mouth and I was enormously impressed by the sound of the siren. When I arrived at the house I saw it was full of people. My mother had invited all the neighbors to celebrate her return from Tunisia. Seeing me, all the women screamed, "*Eeeh*, Lord protect us from the devil," and they fled.

My mother burst out sobbing, "Dirty whore, take a look in the mirror."

I went to the bathroom and saw my neck was covered with hickeys.

To make up for it I wanted to help her prepare the meat to make *kebbe*, which you have to chop very finely. She was cutting the onions and kept repeating, "My God, what a disgrace, I'll never dare to look these women in the face again, it's all the fault of your crazy father who never knew how to raise his daughters, my God, all of West and East Beirut will know about your hickeys."

She wasn't wrong, for all the gossipmongers laughed at the lines of demarcation. After an hour of her sermonizing I couldn't take it anymore. Calmly I got up and pointed the knife at her neck. I can still see the look of terror in her eyes. I think she honestly believed I was going to cut her throat. She fled running. To get away from her fits of weeping, I sought refuge at Maher's. It was raining that night; the shooting was sporadic, and the sea was stormy. The rumbling of the generators covered almost all the noise of the exploding shells. Maher was waiting for me, "What's going on?"

"My mother is treating me like a whore."

"Did you tell her you're still a virgin?"

"She'd never believe me."

"So then you might as well let her be right."

He had sensed my desire to get this thing over and done with. My virginity was weighing heavily on me and I felt I needed to rid myself of it as of a burdensome object, not by making love but in some other way. Maher prepared two lines of cocaine for me. He explained in detail what I had to do and then left me alone. I undressed, turned off the light, lit a bunch of candles, and put on Léo Ferré's "La Mémoire et la Mer." He sang into the night of Beirut, "*La marée, je l'ai dans le cœur qui me remonte. Comme un signe.*" (The tide is in my heart rising like a sign.)

I snorted the first and then the second line. I sat on my haunches, not caressing my vagina, just feeling the thick hair with my fingertips, then I spread my labia and slowly pushed my fingers in. I could hear my father's laughter. I could see Maher's mischievous look. I felt something resistant. I pushed harder. Then I pulled my hand out again and it was red. The door opened, Maher was back. He kissed my eyelids.

Outside the war simply wouldn't stop. That year, the Shiite vigilante group Amal resolved to completely eradicate whatever remained of any Palestinian presence in Beirut. Its soldiers surpassed the Israeli army in their viciousness. Crossing Hamra at night was like playing Russian roulette. From one alley to the next, from one barricade to the next, I risked getting killed, kidnapped, or raped. I would pretend I was drunk, kid around with the militiamen, and when they'd order me to stop I'd answer, "Go ahead, my love, shoot me."

I was playing with fire all the time, for it was our only way to live; when we were with friends we'd talk about only one thing, how each of us had escaped death that day. I started doing coke daily, two dollars a gram; the whole of Beirut was inundated with drugs. I spent my nights dancing at Back Street, where you could find all the children of the war chiefs, the militia, and the children of the political leaders. They were all doing drugs. It was then that I met Nabil, a tall dark-haired guy, who never took off his sunglasses. One evening he suggested we have a nightcap at his place. We drank a lot of whiskey. I sensed he was nervous. He lay down beside me on the couch, then suddenly he got up, threw himself on top of me, and I screamed. We fell down and he nailed me to the floor. He ripped off my dress and my panties. He was breathing hard. I could only see his bloodshot eyes and smell his whiskey breath. He penetrated me. He came in a second and then pulled out. He checked his penis, touched it before examining his fingers and then, furious, he said, "You bitch, you're not a virgin, you bitch, you didn't tell me . . . "

I said nothing, opened the door, and ran. On one side of the coastal road were the Mourabides, on the other the Syrian nationalists, but no one spoke to me, there were no streetlights, and, crying, I moved on through the night. A pack of dogs followed me, I felt the sperm drip down my thighs. Once I got home I wanted to cleanse myself of every trace of him. My panties had stains of blood and sperm. I spent an hour in the shower. I went to my father's study, had a glass of whiskey. I wanted to call him but decided against it, he would never have tolerated it. I drank. I tried to go to bed. That night I felt pregnant. Since abortion was still taboo in Lebanon, I went to see a gynecologist who drew up an official report of rape for me.

Without telling my mother I went to the American Hospital on the eve of my sixteenth birthday to have the pregnancy terminated under general anesthesia. When I woke up I was riddled with terrible pain without knowing what caused it. I was vomiting, shaking, and then the doctors diagnosed a viral infection. I spent ten days in the hospital, went down to eighty-one pounds, and left in a wheelchair.

18

MY PHILOSOPHY OF LIFE WAS VERY simple. I was convinced that I was going to die at any moment, so, hungry for everything, for sex, drugs, and alcohol, I doubled my efforts. I always had a bottle of whiskey in my bag, a pack of cigarettes, and a candle that I would light on the sidewalk on the corner of Makhoul Street where I would spend hours by myself. I wanted to take sexual revenge. I made love like a madwoman, with anyone anywhere. Although I felt nothing I'd do it under porches, on the gravestones of the orthodox cemetery, on the beach, in showers, in cars, and especially in the bathrooms of bars. With a brutality that left no room for desire and even less for any feeling.

I remember Nagy, an effeminate and very refined adolescent who came to see me with a bouquet of flowers and a volume of Paul Eluard's poetry. Without saying a word, I put him down on the couch, took out his penis and straddled him. He was in tears, covered me with kisses, "I was a virgin, Darina, I was a virgin and you've delivered me, I want you to be my wife."

It even made him forget to read me the poem.

One night in July I saw Nabil again, the one who'd raped me, in front of the Mécano. He wanted to save me, keep me from going under, but I snapped at him, "Leave me alone, I'm a free woman."

He didn't take me seriously, "You poor thing, only men are free."

When I heard these words, I turned around and saw a handsome dark guy before me, and said, "You want to get laid?"

He couldn't believe his ears.

"If only . . . "

I took him by the hand, and we went down to the black marble bathroom. I pulled down his pants, gave him a blowjob, then offered him my ass. I pulled away before he could come. He was sitting on the toilet, his belly sprinkled with sperm, and smiled. A few minutes later, he emerged in the bar and ordered champagne for everyone.

At night, I drove around at breakneck speed, headlights off, laying down on the seat with my head under the steering wheel, the bullets whistling through the air, hitting the windows, and I'd be crossing the deserted city to see the clashes at the demarcation line at closer range. Not far from Saint-Georges I met Daoud, a young Shiite vigilante, nineteen years old. We didn't talk about the war, I no longer asked myself any questions like the rest of the world. They kept waging war without even knowing why; they kept waging war just to wage war. We had no ideals, no goals, not even any enemies anymore. Daoud taught me how to navigate Beirut at night, showed me the center of town, the area of the souks where weeds grew two meters tall and where I saw whole families living between the two lines of fire, one hundred meters apart. I liked making love on the demarcation line, in wrecked buildings with their black facade pierced with thousands of bullet holes. I'd lean my hands against the wall and while Daoud was coming inside me I'd read the innumerable graffiti covering the walls of these ruins: To Marika, the whore, forever. To Alya, to death and love. In the distance I'd see the ghostly sea and city and I'd yell to Daoud, "Come, come, come before we die."

In the summer of 1985, I made my decision to become an actress and leave for London to study there. While waiting for the academic year to begin, I spent my days at the beach. One day as I was going across Hamra by car a man ran into me. Right after the collision he jumped out of his car to take one photograph after another of me. His name was Abed, he was a war photographer. Tall and dark, his hair cropped very short like a marine, with black eyes. Impulsive, I slept with him that very night. It was the first time I made love on a bed with sheets and the light on. I believe I'd never seen the face of my other partners, that's how dark it always was. I didn't know what a caress was or what a man's arms felt like.

Thanks to him, I very rapidly entered the world of the press in Beirut. I was living with him in a building where only other war photographers lived, who came home haggard every night just to drink until dawn before going back to the front. After a week of living together, Abed asked for my hand. My mother was against it and so I left to be with my father in Nicosia for the Christmas holidays. He came along with me on my nocturnal jaunts, dancing like Travolta. I told him everything, kept nothing secret from him. He always had his nose in his glass and would listen without ever uttering a word of judgment. He laughed at my amorous adventures. I'd describe in detail the sex organs of each partner I'd straddled, sucked, or satisfied by hand. But the drugs scared him. Abed was supposed to join us the next day, very eager to meet my father. He stood on the balcony and from the second floor watched Abed ring the doorbell. He took his coat, put on his hat, and said, "See you later, daughter, this guy is a piece of shit, I'd be careful if I were you."

I knew that he was never wrong where people were concerned but I swore to him that he'd never see me again if he didn't welcome my suitor. Reluctantly he stayed but didn't say a word throughout the entire meeting.

The idea of my marriage didn't enthrall him. As he took me to the airport he warned me, "My girl, if you want to have an experience with that man go ahead, but watch out, do not get married. I want to make you into a liberated woman, not a subservient one."

I returned to Beirut only to go back to the hospital again. My oldest sister Rana had just left her fiancé who was becoming more and more fundamentalist. The night she broke up with him, she was partying and happily rediscovering the pleasures of alcohol. As she was going back to Hamra, the militia shot her tires. The car overturned and Rana flew through the windshield. She was scalped by the pieces of glass. Before taking her to the operating room, the doctor asked me to leave because it was going to be an unbearable spectacle. I told him that I'd been working with the Red Cross for years and that nothing shocked me anymore, for I'd seen so many horrors. I helped him shave my sister. She came out of it with seventy-nine stitches. In the emergency room this was par for the course, every vigilante wanted to have his wounded treated before any others. The doctors operated first and foremost on those who had the most weapons and dollars. If you had neither you died in the street.

I was determined to get married. In the city I was being called every name under the sun and thought I would become a respectable woman once I was married. Because of the fighting the Ministry of Education had offered the baccalaureate diploma to everyone in the graduating class. I'd found work as a continuity girl at the TV station. Abed needed money to rent an apartment. Thanks to my father's friends, he managed to do a story on the clandestine training camps in the Bekaa Plains. The scoop brought in seventy thousand francs, a fortune for him. We rented a large apartment in Hamra. I went along with him to cover a story on the cultivation of hashish in Bekaa. Right after Chtaura, the entire valley was one immense field of cannabis. Just opening the car windows was enough to have the smell waft in. It was harvest time and there weren't enough local pickers, so the Lebanese farmers were recruiting Syrian and Jordanian Bedouins. You could see their brightly colored scarves dancing amid the cannabis in the green fields. Everyone smoked. The "Lebanese" was considered to be the best. It was the poorest region in Lebanon but within a few years every farmer was driving a Mercedes. At every village entrance there were barricades and Syrian armored vehicles that exacted payment on the most insignificant bundle. The farmers in the region of Hermel had begun to cultivate opium and made it into cocaine on the spot. We spent two weeks with all the war reporters who were there for one long tasting session.

I watched Abed use cocaine and LSD but I'd decided never to use any in front of him. Somehow I had a premonition that it would overpower me. His parents were very different from mine: his mother was veiled and his father prayed day and night. In their house, the carpet was covered in plastic, and in the kitchen the handles of the pots were wrapped in aluminum foil to prevent their wear and tear.

Since Lebanese law requires that all individuals be married according to the rituals of their own faith, we were married before a sheikh at the Sunni court.

We celebrated our nuptials in January 1986 in a restaurant in Hamra. When we came home he wanted to make love, but since he'd used a lot of cocaine he couldn't get it up. I was naked. He was holding his sagging penis in one hand, trying desperately to get it hard, and with the other he was dealing me blow after blow. That evening I came to see a different side of him.

From that first day on, our sex life shifted and became a systematic rape. He duplicated every one of his mother's tics—for instance, I wasn't to leave any fingerprints on the chrome handle of the refrigerator. When he saw the slightest trace of one he'd drag me by my hair to the living room.

He turned into a cleanliness maniac and carried within him all the violence of the war, increased tenfold; he'd jump for joy at every explosion, dreaming of making the print of his life. It was the time when the liberation of the French hostages was under negotiation. Abed spent his nights in hotel lobbies gathering statements from his sources, while I was doing sound recording for foreign TV correspondents.

I discovered true violence while hanging out with these war reporters. We had transformed one bedroom into a darkroom, he taught me how to develop film, and these were the only moments of tenderness when, in the dark, I was developing photographs of corpses, destruction, and weaponry. We became very violent with each other. Sometimes he'd come home from covering a story after nights of combat and I'd expose his rolls of film to the bright daylight while he was in the shower. He hated sleeping on crumpled sheets and forced me to attach them to the reverse side of the mattress with straight pins, so that night after night my fingers were bleeding.

Abed slept around and gave me all sorts of infections. I went to see the gynecologist who discovered I was pregnant and was shocked. She asked him to abstain or use a condom. He swore he'd take every precaution. The next day he came home drugged and took me in his arms. I thought he was going to embrace me, but he put his hand on my genitals. I pushed him away. I was busy pinning down the sheets and had pushed the top of the bed so I could get around it, when he flew into a mad rage. He saw that I was caught between the base of the bed and the wall, and with his full weight he thrust it against my belly. I screamed but he didn't hear me. Again he'd taken out his penis and was masturbating and at the same time kicking hard against the base of the bed. I felt something explode inside my belly, ran to the bathroom, and laid down in the tub with blood pouring profusely from my vagina. I didn't move, said nothing, simply listened to my body at last emptying itself of all his brutality. He opened the door, saw the scene, and fled. I had the stamina to phone my mother who took me straight to the hospital. Under the influence of the anesthesia, I began to tell her everything: the beatings, the repeated rape, the sodomy, the drugs. I opened my eyes and saw my mother's face wet with tears.

Abed came to pick me up. He begged me on his knees to come back to him. I told myself that I should give him a chance. That same night he took me in his arms and I let myself go, put my head against his chest, and again he put his hand on my genitals. I pushed him away, he raised his hand to hit me, but then I took out my father's gun, "If you touch me I'll blow your brains out."

I asked for a divorce. He threatened to put me in a "house of surrender." In Islam, when a husband lodges a complaint against his wife for desertion, the police forcibly bring her back and the husband can "tame her" by locking her up at home or in a stairwell. That evening I went to see some friends in the militia in Ouzaï to give them Abed's address. I asked them how much it would cost to have him eliminated. "Twenty-five cents, Darina, you just pay the price of the bullet."

I announced my plan to him. He sent me the divorce papers the next day.

19 AFTER MY DIVORCE I FOUND WORK AT the radio and TV station again. I was earning a lot of money. I spent a great deal of time at the university in Hamra, where I felt the

pressure of the Islamists. My theater group was rehearsing *La Conférence des oiseaux*. The bearded men came into the theater, put their prayer mats on the stage, and prostrated themselves facing Mecca. I kicked them in the ass. Sacrilege. There were eight of them, they beat me up, and broke everything in sight.

My mother was frequently in Cyprus to be with my father, Rana had found a husband, and Nayla was in Brussels. I was alone, using more than eight grams of coke a day, costing two hundred dollars a kilo.

It was the period when Christians were being slaughtered by the Druzes. In a mountain I found bodies of naked women tied up in barbed wire. Our thirst for blood had no limits anymore, and cocaine no longer had any effect on me, so I decided to move on to freebase. In Ouzaï there was a shantytown much like the Palestinian fields where you'd find illegals, drugs, and weapons. The Mercedes-Benzes of the bourgeoisie were lined up in front of one of the hovels where they came to shop. It was the shop of the cocaine king, Abou Ali. After going through a heavy steel double door I found myself in a large living room with people sitting on mattresses on the floor. He taught me the art of transforming coke into freebase: take a soup spoon, put in the pure cocaine with a pinch of baking soda and a drop of water. After readying a glass of water and some ice cubes, you light a lighter underneath the spoon, and the powder turns into oil. Quickly extinguish the flame and let any excess drops of water drip off the spoon until the oil becomes hard as a rock. Then you take a plastic bottle of water and turn it into a hookah. You light the cocaine, placed on a bit of aluminum foil, and you inhale the smoke. You hold your breath and try to keep the smoke in as long as you possibly can before exhaling. I followed his directions to the letter, felt as if the blood was spurting from my skull and an immense draft was rushing through my body, as if I were leaving my body, as if I were emptying myself of myself.

I met Ramzi, a twenty-six-year-old musician who had a small apartment in Hamra. We were together all the time. The war was there but, numb and indifferent, we no longer saw it. We were on a perpetual overdose of violence. Insensitive, or better yet, needing to be in hot places, dangerous corners, we ran toward the bullets like moths to the light. Afraid of running into Abed, I was never without my Smith & Wesson. It was April and Beirut's blue trees were in bloom. I was at Ramzi's with Hussein, a young student waiting for his emigration visa for the United States. We'd used thirty grams of coke in forty-eight hours without sleeping. Janis Joplin was playing in a continuous loop.

Ramzi played the guitar; late in the night he had a brainstorm, "How about playing Russian roulette?"

I laughed and immediately agreed. Hussein wasn't up for it but didn't want to chicken out in front of us. Ramzi was excited, "Here's the rule, whoever loses leaves his dose to the next one, and even if someone dies we play on. A hit is more important than death."

Ramzi picked up my gun. He was singing "I Will Survive," his eyes were shimmering, and he took his dose of freebase. Slowly he put the barrel to his temple. I was watching him, fascinated. At moments like this everything goes on in the eyes. I could feel his exhilaration and at the same time I was exhilarated. I finally understood how you can outdistance death, overtake it even, not be at the mercy of a stray bullet any longer, but at the mercy of oneself.

I saw how you can pass death at the finish line. Slowly Ramzi pulled the trigger, no bullet. He was alive. He jumped up, laughing wildly, "This is beyond belief, free base is like Laughing Cow cheese compared to Russian roulette."

I picked up the gun, took out the bullet, and put it in a different chamber before turning the barrel. An eternity goes by between the moment you put the cold barrel against your temple and the moment your finger moves to the trigger. Inside my head, I heard a voice yelling at me louder and louder, "Come on now, go ahead, what are you waiting for, what are you waiting for, what are you waiting for, just pull!" I pulled, I was alive. I leaped up, I shouted, I felt as if someone had opened my chest with one blow to rip out my heart. Hussein took the gun from my hands, but right at the moment he was going to pull the trigger, he broke down and dissolved in tears, crying that he didn't want to die. We felt sorry for him.

I was drenched, sweating from head to toe, dripping wet. I had to wait at least half an hour before my fingers were dry enough to pick up my weapon again.

Hussein kept repeating mechanically that we were mad, that he was leaving for the United States forever to get away from this shitty country. I laughed at his terror. "Coward, you can't leave the most beautiful country in the world."

It was Ramzi's turn. He was sitting cross-legged on the floor; I got on all fours to watch him close up. I put my face near his. Our eyes locked, our faces glued to each other, our lips touching. I told him, "You look like Robert de Niro in *The Deer Hunter.*"

He took the gun without turning the barrel and with a strange smile he kept humming:

First I was afraid
I was petrified

Kept thinking I could never live
without you by my side
But I spent so many nights
thinking how you did me wrong
I grew str . . .

He pulled. His brain spurted out on my hair. Crumpled in his corner, Hussein was shrieking at the top of his lungs. I picked up the song where Ramzi had left off.

. . . grew strong
I learned how to carry on
and so you're back
from outer space
I just walked in to find you here

I opened his left hand, I took his dose, and kept on. as he had said, the most important thing is to keep playing. "The hit is more important than death."

20 ON OCTOBER 23, 1989, I WAS IN DAMAScus, living a passionate love story. I'd been married for a year to Adel, an emotive actor, frail and jealous, who could only make love in the dark. That night we had danced at the Cham Palace, where he'd been drinking. He had collapsed in

his underwear and was snoring softly. I couldn't sleep, was gazing at the stone walls, the carpet on the floor. I wanted to go out and just walk but since I always got lost in the maze of the old city, I decided against it. I got up to go to the kitchen and make some personal-style Nescafé: a pinch of the powder, nothing else, and half a liter of water. I turned on the radio very quietly to hear the four o'clock news and this flash: "Today all the Lebanese parties meeting in Taef, Saudi Arabia, have agreed to a peace accord." My first thought was leaving Adel. Initially I thought that the peace accord was a joke; every day for fifteen years the war had been supposed to stop. I got dressed, packed my bags, and took a taxi for Beirut.

In Beirut nothing had really changed—I found the same piles of garbage and the same roaming packs of dogs. It felt strange to walk the city streets without the militia shouting and the noise of bullets. It would take just a few days for the city's features to be completely transformed. Everyone was so eager to turn the page, to forget the 150 thousand who had died for nothing. The snipers, the gunmen, the assassins melted away into the crowd in no time. An army of assassins vanished into thin air with a wave of the magic wand called amnesia. The war had created more than three hundred thousand wounded but there was not a disabled person to be seen in the streets. Lebanese society was ashamed of its handicapped citizens; it had hidden them or blotted them out like a misspelling. Everyone had turned the page very fast, without reading it. The Lebanese disposed of their war history like a dead body.

I made the rounds of all Hamra to find an apartment but no landlord wanted to rent to "a young unmarried woman." I went over to the East where I met Dany, a Greek Catholic. He was a well-known homosexual but my father was intrigued by our relationship.

"You're not in Paris, but in Beirut where the people are very nasty."

People often called out at me in the street, "So, no more men in Beirut so now you're fucking a queer?"

Dany lived in Badaro, not far from the museum, one of the hottest spots during the war. He wanted to convert to Islam, while I was wearing a turquoise crucifix and crossed myself in every church. He loved making love and I would spend entire afternoons with him. Our bedroom had a large, very wide wooden bed. The windows were closed all the time because of the joint across the street where they played clandestine poker games around the clock. There were rugs on the floor that I'd brought back from my stays in all the Arab capitals where I'd shown a film on the condition of women. I would always put on Nina Simone before undressing, running a bath for myself, lighting candles, and Dany would always make the tub overflow. I'd watch his hands caressing my thighs under the water and his fingers getting lost in my heart-shaped vagina. I'd get out of the tub all wet and he'd lick me dry. I liked his long, big, circumcised penis hard in my mouth. Dany suffered from a serious skin disease. I have never liked handsome men. At the moment of orgasm, our moans were inevitably covered by the cries from the poker games.

"Three of a kind, queens, *y a maniak!*"

"Royal flush, *y a ars!*"

The city was being rebuilt; it was open and I could go anywhere. We were in such a hurry to make peace, we forgot that the southern half of the country was still occupied by the Israelis. The country was split between those who had experienced the war and those who had left. We blamed them for fleeing, while they weren't coming to terms with the fact that they'd missed the great old war years. To notify us that "depravity" had come to an end, the government had passed a law that forbade men to have women on their laps in public.

My mother then begged me to get married, as I was at the mercy of all sorts of police raids.

We were married in the Greek Orthodox Church. I'd been baptized in a church in Aleppo, Syria, but in the eyes of the priest I wasn't Christian enough and he re-baptized me Greek Orthodox and gave me the name Marie. I believed that with this marriage I would finally resolve my documentation problems. What bliss! I ran to the registry office with my baptismal certificate but the officer explained that since I was Syrian, I had to register my marriage in Syria. I went to Damascus but there they told me that I was considered to be Muslim and that my marriage to a Christian was strictly forbidden by "my religion." I remembered that Dany had a certificate of conversion to Islam, signed by an imam of the venerated Al-Azhar Mosque in Cairo. But then we had to return to Beirut to have his conversion validated by the registry office, which refused under the pretext that such a procedure would endanger the equilibrium between the communities!

Things with Dany were disintegrating very rapidly. He would follow me at night, rummage through my belongings, and sniff my panties for the scent of another man. I asked my father what my attitude ought to be. He was categorical, "If ever a man, no matter who he is, assaults your freedom as a woman, repudiate him without giving it another thought."

I made an appointment with the priest who informed me that the Church did not allow divorce, no exceptions made, but for ten thousand he might be able to make things easier for me. I went to the tribunal of the Roman Catholics. The priest was waiting for me, and said, "Where are the greenbacks?"

I gave him the bag. He handed it to a novice in a cassock who was to count the bills. As he waited for the result, the priest read the Gospel of St. Mark and when he heard the words "it's fine," he gave me a certificate of annulment without so much as a word.

I returned to my single life. Not wanting to see Beirut in the bright light of day, I lived in the dark with the drapes drawn all day long. I wasn't able to live without the war anymore, my body had been programmed for it ever since childhood. Fear had fine-tuned me and all my gestures made sense only in relationship to that fear—how to steer clear of walls and windows, listen to noise, sniff danger, cross a street— none of it made any sense anymore in a time of peace. Cut off from war I no longer knew how to love, how to screw. I couldn't sleep without the muttering sound of bullets. From one day to the next I decided to wage war against myself, as if I had no further interest in anything anymore. In the street, as I watched other people, I was constantly wondering which of them had killed and which of them hadn't, who had raped and who hadn't. When I would fuck militiamen on the demarcation line I used to know what I was doing and who was what. After the war they all put on the same mask, executioners and victims mingling. I went to bed at seven in the morning and got up around five in the afternoon to have a glass of whiskey and wait for night to fall, for the sky to turn bluish-black before I went out. I lived in Achrafieh. I couldn't really go west anymore, I didn't want to see my city peaceful. Sometimes I'd go to Hamra surreptitiously. I was scared, as if I was no longer allowed to sit on the beach, as if there wasn't any room for me anymore there where I belonged because I had stayed and hadn't left like the rest of them. I went back to cocaine, now up to one hundred dollars a gram, I'd snort $500 worth per night, the average Lebanese salary.

When gunshots woke me up one morning, I quickly slipped on a dress, jubilant because I thought the war was back and, being its orphan, I had been waiting every night for its return. But the concierge brought me down to earth, "It's nothing, the city has ordered all the dogs to be killed. They've eaten too many Lebanese."

There would be no dogs left in Beirut.

Censorship was reinstated: synopses of movies and scripts of theater plays had to be submitted to the office of control. It was illegal to allude to any religions or religious denominations. In television series first names with a strongly religious association were prohibited, such as Michél or Mohammed; Rami or Samy had to be used instead. The police often made the rounds of the libraries to remove books that were considered to be subversive.

In the center of Beirut, heavy-duty construction equipment was demolishing the heart of the city. The Hariri Company completed the work of what the war had left standing, costing millions of dollars. In a matter of months, the historic core of Beirut was razed to the ground, leaving behind a piece of wasteland and empty, expensive facades. As empty as our memories.

My father very clearly saw that I was drifting. He sensed that I wasn't handling my failed love life very well. One night when he had been drinking a bit, he had a brilliant idea, "Tell me, since things never worked out with men, why not try women, perhaps that's where you'll find your happiness?"

I thought of Aline, a brunette with green eyes, an almost transparent white skin, and curly chestnut hair, whose eyes devoured me every night at the Babylon. She was exciting, and we both had balls. That very evening I reserved a table for two at the Babylon. I caressed her openly in public. She almost died with fear. I talked to her about how much I wanted to make love to her, and kissed her on the mouth while the waiters were watching us thunderstruck.

We took a room at the Palmyra in Baalbek. We danced amid the ruins. We saw the sun come up above the temple of Bacchus and glow on the snow of Mount Lebanon. We went up to our room located in an old Lebanese building, its high walls covered with canvases and drawings by Cocteau, and its old furniture uphol-stered in Oriental silk. There were two very large brass beds with white sheets and lace pillowcases.

It was as if I were starting all over again—the first kiss of my life, the first gentle touch; I felt as if I lived in another century in my wide white abaya. We were very intimidated. She began to tenderly stroke my face and neck. I was wearing a low-cut nightgown. We drew closer to each other, our lips barely touching, our tongues ended up entwined, almost paralyzed by our desire. She didn't want me touching her but her fingers gently brushed my breasts, my belly, then burying her-self between my legs she opened my labia and caressed me with her mouth, her fingers. I felt her tongue on my clitoris, and yet I felt nothing. I don't know how much time she spent kissing my belly and my genitals but I felt nothing; I was aware of the beauty of the act, of the splendor of her woman's body on top of mine. I was staring out the open window at the cypresses bending in the wind; in the distance I heard the morning call to prayer. I was getting wet in her mouth and her lips but I couldn't come, and told myself that I must love men too much.

Of course, I called my father to tell him the story. "Well, my girl, now do you know who you are?"

"No, Papa, it's too soon to tell."

In the meantime my father's papers had expired. The only choice he had was to go to Damascus to obtain his passport. Together with my mother I went to the person in charge of the Syrian Secret Service who was then running Lebanon. He welcomed us with open arms and laughed at our anxiety, "What are you afraid of? You make me laugh—you must be living on some other planet to be having such nightmares. Syria is not some big bad wolf, don't let him worry, he'll be treated there with all the honors his rank deserves."

He handed us a paper with his signature on it.

In Damascus my father was supposed to go to the "Palestinian" section where he was interrogated from early morning to late afternoon; they let him come home to us to sleep. After ten days of interrogation he disappeared. I spent two weeks knocking on the doors of every police bureau and information office. Toward the end one officer received me to say that I'd better leave Syria if I didn't want to join my father, who told me later that they had locked him up in a glass cell. They hadn't touched him but they had installed loudspeakers broadcasting the screams of prisoners they were torturing day and night.

After forty days in prison my father was set free. A few days later his brother Samy died. Again we begged the people in Damascus to let him attend the funeral of his oldest brother, but this time they made it clear to us that he wouldn't be permitted to be on Syrian territory at all. Deeply hurt by this sentence, he had a heart attack, and I stayed by his side until he had open heart surgery. He held my hand before asking me, "If I die, bury me in Salamiyeh."

Recently he had become quite aware that all his dreams of liberty, secularity, and love had gone up in smoke. He knew that he had lost. When the nurses came for him, he kissed me, "Daughter, if you're here only because of me, I'm going to die to make your task easier, but do not stay in this city."

21 THE PHONE RANG IN THE MIDDLE OF the night. Before I answered it I knew that my father had died. It was raining. I didn't see anything of the city.

All Beirut was at my parents' house: military, journalists, politicians, and even Palestinian refugees who were living underground, some of them from abroad.

We left for Arnoun the next day, forming a convoy

of several cars with my father in an ambulance. It was very cold and raining, the soil was red and soaked, its smell rising to the sky on the coastal road. The sea was covered by a quiet fog; the world seemed cleansed. I opened the window, and smelled the scent of the rain and the deep green grass that resembled that of freshly cut pistachios. I saw it all again, the paths where we smoked our first cigarette, the road the Volvo had taken, and the Château de Beaufort I couldn't enter because of twenty years of occupation. Grandfather's house had been destroyed by the Israeli army. We found shelter in an uncle's house, where we stayed for the time it took the gravediggers to do their job. We lay my father on the table in the kitchen whose walls had been gutted by the bombs. Before the noon prayer the men came to pick up my father. There was a sheikh to say the prayer of the dead.

I cried out, "Stop! He didn't want any prayers."

The men pushed me aside, "Come on, let go! Women are not allowed at any burial."

They buried him as Muslim tradition requires, on his right side with his face turned toward Mecca. It was all over in a minute's time. The men wandered off and I stayed behind, alone at the grave site. Strange to think that he had asked me to have him buried with his face turned toward the crusaders' castle, "With great fanfare, my daughter, with saxophones and trumpets." I sifted through the fresh earth, mumbling the same phrase, "Now that you're no longer here, to whom am I going to tell my stories?"

I didn't want to stay in the village and went back to Beirut. That evening I felt like going out, like having a drink to him. I went to the Babylon, ordered a Bloody Mary without any alcohol, asked the DJ to put on "Sinner Man" by Nina Simone, and went out onto the dance floor. I don't know why I felt like taking off my T-shirt and exposing my breasts, but I felt a hand grab me by the hair. It was the man who had played the cassette of the Koran and he had six thugs with him. They dragged me around the floor three times, while everyone pretended not to see and moved aside to let them through. I was screaming. I couldn't believe what was happening. The men turned their eyes away as if they didn't know me. For all my friends of twenty years' standing, I didn't exist anymore. They stepped over me and kept dancing to the music of Nina Simone. Some were applauding, "She thought she was a star, it's good that a man is putting her in her place."

Still dragging me by the hair, they yanked me down a stone staircase. I could feel my ribs being crushed against the steps. I was still screaming. No one budged in the club where I'd spent almost my entire youth. The men reassured the patrons, "Her father didn't bring her up right, we're going to reeducate her."

On the terrace, a girl who was in the theater called out, "That's Madame Darina!"

They pushed her aside viciously. Once in the street they tried to force me into a car. I reared up and kicked back, breaking the car door window. Then they went berserk and put my head in the gutter. A bouncer tried to intervene, "You're crazy beating up a chick like that; let her go."

One of the men answered, "You know what this bitch did?"

"No?"

"She said that the Koran was shit."

The bouncer grabbed me and put me in a headlock, "Get her now, brothers, I've got the bitch."

They kept battering me with their fists. I tried to protect my face, felt my mouth filling with blood. Then they stood me up against a gate whose bars were wrapped with barbed wire. I felt the metal spikes ripping my back. Then I crumpled and before blacking out felt them stomping on my body and face. Nayla arrived yelling, snatched me from their hands, and took me home.

I opened my eyes. I was home, hurled to the floor. The first thing I thought of was to run to the bathroom to see what they had done to me. In front of the mirror I carefully raised my head, pretending to be a camera, to be the mirror. When I saw my reflection, I shouted, "Papa, those sons of bitches!"

I didn't recognize myself: my right eye had burst open and was bluish mauve, the nerves were completely torn. Blood was flowing from my ear, two ribs were broken, and I had mud on my face. My back was shredded from the barbed wire. My lip was split, the arch of my eyebrow was lacerated, my jaw was fractured, and my eyes looked like my father's the day after he'd been attacked. My mother arrived in the middle of the night, keeping her eyes lowered because she didn't dare look at me. I was shouting, seeing faces in a blur, everything dancing in front of my eyes. Since I couldn't move anymore, they decided to take me to the hospital, I don't remember how we got there, I don't remember the car, but we made it to the Greek Orthodox Hospital. I laughed when I saw the shoe prints on my belly; they admitted me to the emergency room. They took X-rays; my ribs were broken, but the tests showed no trace of any cocaine or alcohol in my blood.

The nurses who knew me were astounded, "Madame Darina, is this makeup for a new role?"

The doctor announced that they'd have to keep me

overnight to weather the shock. Once in my room I phoned all my friends to tell them the story. Around four o'clock the nurses took away my cell phone and unplugged the landline. A few minutes later, three gigantic men with mustaches burst into my room, one of them with a syringe in his hand; I asked him what it was and he told me it was just a tranquillizer to help me sleep. When I saw them come at me, I bolted from the bed, but they caught up with me in the hallway. They flattened me to the floor. I felt the shot. My eyes closed instantly; it was the black hole. I don't know how long I slept but when I woke up I saw I was in a car. Dawn was breaking over Beirut, looking very yellow because of the magnesium street lights. I tried to scratch my head but couldn't. It seemed I was trussed up: they had me in a straitjacket. I saw my mother, my sisters, and an uncle in the distance. Their faces seemed huge. I watched the walls, the buildings. I heard the road workers. I couldn't speak. My mouth tasted like blood. I had only two questions in my head: Does my father know what's happening to me? What would he do if he saw the condition I'm in? I dozed off again. When I opened my eyes the second time I was in a room, strapped to a steel table. There was a cold white light, a male nurse with a mustache, and a female nurse wearing a nun's cap. In her hand was a syringe, aimed at me, and she said in alarm, "Careful, she's waking up. We need to give her a shot, we need to give her a shot."

I wanted to say something but the shot came too fast.

Surfacing hours later, I was still tied down, to a bed this time. The linoleum-covered walls were yellow, and the window had bars on it. Above my head were a large crucifix and an icon of the Virgin. I smelled disgusting. I had peed on myself and vomited up all the morphine on my belly.

I had no idea where I was. The nun came over to me, trembling as if I were some wild animal. I begged her to tell me where I was, at least. She finally answered me, "You're mad and you're in the women's hospital for the insane in Jounieh."

The next day I found myself sitting in a chair in a huge room, in my straitjacket. The windowpanes were opaque. A row of green leather couches stood along the walls, bouquets of plastic flowers were covered in dust, and pictures of the Virgin were everywhere. In a corner a television set suspended from the wall was broadcasting video clips in Arabic. With every move I made, the nuns slapped me. In the back of the room, strange women were holding Christian rosaries and praying while they watched TV.

The oldest one came over to kiss me and said, "I'm delighted to meet you, Glub Pasha."

Another slightly younger one had a game that consisted of going from one woman to another and farting in her face. She smelled like a corpse. All the women looked more than one hundred years old and as if they'd been there for centuries. I recognized a familiar face in the group; it was Zeïna who used to dance with me at *Back Street*. She had recognized me as well. She stroked my hair and speaking to me in English she whispered, "If you want to get out of here alive, accept your state of craziness."

I spent the day restrained, watching all these mad women. I saw them all and understood that I was paying the price for my insane female liberty in this country of madmen. I understood that I should do everything they wanted.

They woke us up at six in the morning to take a shower. We were lined up naked; closing the doors was forbidden. The tubs were black, the windowpanes broken. There was no hot, only ice-cold water; the nurses would frisk us all the time. It was cold, and my body was blue. Because of the medication, I was peeing on myself every day and to punish me they forced me to clean the toilets. The bowls were always clogged and you had to clean them out with a broomstick. I slept in the straitjacket that the nurses put on me at nine o'clock sharp in the evening. On the third day I met the psychiatrist who informed me that my family was complaining about me because I talked too much, I laughed a lot, and I danced too much. Innocently, I answered, "Yes, I talk too much because sometimes I see things and I hear things."

He reacted with horror, "You hear things?"

I knew I'd made a mistake.

"No, doctor, I swear, I don't hear anything, I don't take anything, I don't see anything."

As he was writing a prescription for a tranquilizer for the dangerously insane, he warned me, "All right, but promise me that you won't say anything to the mother superior about the beatings you're getting. Nobody has hit you, nobody has struck you."

I was received by the mother superior in a minuscule room with a leather and metal desk, and a Bakelite telephone. A World War II setting. Gospels everywhere, pictures of the Virgin, and metal cabinets with cardboard binders. Sister Simone, a huge woman dressed in white with a large silver cross around her neck, explained to me that I was not allowed to make phone calls or to go into the garden by myself. I was there only to rest, to sleep, and to get fresh air to get my health back.

The tables in the refectory were made of steel and covered with waterproof canvas cloths. Meals were served from large bowls. The nuns had given me permission not to eat meat, and I made do with boiled potatoes and stale bread. We were forbidden to throw up any food or to refuse a dish. Next to the balcony was a small smoking room and I was allowed two cigarettes a day, which I smoked down to the very stub. No one in my family had shown up. My mother sent me clothes with a driver named Georges who threw the bundles at me before he raced off. One day I came across one of my gay friends, a doctor, and I ran over to him to have him help me, but he pushed me away and said, "Go away, don't tell them you know me or they'll think that I'm just like you."

I spent hours in the television room watching the women, some of whom were very calm and not at all crazy. In the end I found out that they were locked up there at the request of their families. Camille, who owned some buildings in the Eighth Arrondissement in Paris, had been committed by her family, who wanted to take control of her property. Anna had been there for months at the request of her husband who wanted to marry someone else. One day they admitted Leila, a girl from Baalbek, the "Muslim girl" as the nurses called her. She, too, was there at her husband's request, who wanted to take a second wife. As soon as she put on her veil and picked up her mat to say her prayers, the nuns rushed over to her, hit her, and put her in a straitjacket. She was beautiful with her huge eyes, and implored them, "Sisters, I love you, I love you."

I myself played the good Christian, spending hours on my knees in front of the statue of the Virgin. You had to be willing to do anything to be crazy. I was afraid of playing the game—of accepting madness—and then truly becoming mad. I felt lonely. I was lonely. I would wake up at night and, since writing was not allowed, I would look at the sky and write letters to my father with my finger in the air. I was knocked out by the drugs. I walked with my head down. I smiled like the rest of them. In addition to morphine injections, the nurses gave me pills when I woke up, again at noon, and again at night. The convent was divided into four floors, of which the first one was for wealthy women who were there for detoxification, the second for minor problems, the third for serious cases, such as mine, and the basement for raging madwomen. At night I would hear the women in the basement shrieking as they were being beaten. On the fifteenth day the psychiatrist came to see me. "It seems that your conduct is irreproachable, your health is improving, you are obedient, and take all your medications without any problem. Keep up the good work and your family will come to visit you this afternoon in the park."

The Convent of the Cross, the hospital for insane women, overlooks the bay of Jounieh. There was an enormous pine tree, and I was sitting on a stone bench. Then I heard a car engine. A taxi dropped my mother off. She sat down across from me on a bench. I wanted to kiss her but with a nod of his head the psychiatrist told me not to. I controlled myself. I shouldn't scream, shouldn't raise my voice: it was important to give the impression that I had been permanently tamed. My mother was smiling. I had my head down, a beatific smile on my face. She looked at me and seemed happy. She asked, "Daughter, are you happy?"

"Yes, Mama, I am very happy, thanks to you."

At that point, the psychiatrist who was present throughout the meeting told me, "We all agree on one thing, we will let you go under the condition that you stop going out, stop dancing, stop drinking, stop staying up all night, or else we'll have you committed again and bring you back here, understood?"

I played up my bliss, smiled, acquiesced, "Yes, doctor, yes, doctor, yes, doctor, I swear I will."

I was watching my mother and the psychiatrist. Criminals. Who told you that I won't kill myself? Do you have any idea how many screams I've suppressed so as not to go mad, not to die like a dog? For the first time in my life I felt the fear of being abandoned and of being left there for good. I played the entire film of my life, all the scenes with my father, all the men I had known, all the cities I'd walked, and I could hear my father laughing when he'd say, "It is forbidden to forbid."

I'd never known any fear, not at the worst moments of the war. I used to joke around beneath the F-16s. I used to dance while the most horrible massacres were taking place. I would make love while bombs were falling, but at the Convent of the Cross I was shaking all the time. I was afraid of the beatings of the nuns, afraid to pee, afraid of having to wash the toilets. The women I saw around me were the same as the women I'd seen in the Arab world: beasts of burden. I had understood our vulnerability as women: it's fine to be a star, a doctor, a celebrity, but at the slightest misstep a woman becomes a woman again, a beast of burden who is tied up as men see fit. I was afraid of myself. I knew that I could play the role of the madwoman and would run the risk of being one for good; actually, that was even easier for me than confronting this society that knew only how to make their people live with a sense of shame. I had decided to live. I would have to make compromises, and at the same time I had to play their game. I wanted to get out of the tunnel, go toward the light. All my freedom was nothing but an illusion; it was in fact easier for me to stay with these crazy women who truly loved me.

I thought of Soumaya who was in love with me, who threw herself at me, and bit me till I bled. It was easier to live with her than with Beirut's society where my back was covered with labels—druggie, whore, madwoman, lesbian, atheist . . .

I had packed all my things in a garbage bag. The walls were gray blue, the air smelled of the cold and of death. I arrived on the ground floor. No one in my family had dared to come and see where I was: no one knew which bed was mine, from which zinc bowl I ate.

I was so happy to have put together a collage of video clips with the women. The same songs showed in a continuous loop. The women had learned them by heart. We had made a karaoke.

I slept with my shoes on while waiting for my liberation. The next day no one appeared to liberate me. The mother superior wanted to give me a present, "My daughter, I give you permission to go and get bread at the convent bakery."

How proud I was! I carried the baguettes as if they were gold ingots. Since I hadn't heard a word from my family, I begged an assistant to lend me his phone so I could call my sister. He was afraid. "Listen, I'll leave the phone over there on the table and I'll say that someone stole it."

On the other end of the line my mother was very

embarrassed, "We can't sign you out just yet, your committal has cost $7,000 and I don't have that amount."

The nightmare wasn't over yet. I called an old friend who had made a fortune during the war. He sent me the money within the hour, only insisting that I reimburse him in kind.

I crossed the threshold and my family was waiting. I didn't believe I was free. I pretended to kiss my mother.

I was afraid I'd cry and that she, seeing my tears, would take me back to the asylum. The psychiatrist had warned me: anyone who spends time at the convent is registered as having been an inmate. Any member of that person's family can alert the police concerning his or her conduct, at any time, and the person will be recommitted.

My mother had my required remedies on her lap: boxes of Lithium—six tablets, ten milligrams each—and Rivotril—six tablets, ten milligrams each—to be taken every day.

I had always thought that, with all its filth and shit, Beirut was the most beautiful city in the world, but as I came out that day I didn't have the slightest feeling for, the slightest attachment to this place that no longer existed in my eyes; I had erased myself completely from its streets, its walls, its sea. In fact, I was paying the bill for thirty years of imaginary freedom in this city of hypocrites, lies, and greasepaint. There was a monstrous traffic jam on the highway. The Lebanese drive the same way they make love: very badly. My mother was repeating the psychiatrist's instructions to me, "You promise not to dance anymore, not to drink or smoke anymore, not to go out with men anymore, not to talk the way you did before, or else . . . "

I was looking at the city that seemed like a vast prison to me. Inside my head all Beirut had turned into the Convent of the Cross, as if they had grafted bars onto my eyes. I nodded my head to let her know I agreed with everything.

I had died at the Convent of the Cross and stayed there. I was born on the day I left it.

The next day I was at the airport looking for a flight to London but every plane was fully booked. There was one seat on a flight to Paris. I grabbed it. Paris, may I never leave you.

DARINA AL-JOUNDI was born in Lebanon in 1968 to a Shiite Lebanese mother and a secular Syrian father. She began her acting career at age eight with Lebanese television. At thirty, she left Beirut for Paris, where she wrote and performed *Le jour où Nina Simone a cessé de chanter* for the theater. The play caused a sensation at the Avignon Festival, where it was hailed by critics all over France. Her latest movie, *Un homme perdu*, by Danielle Arbid, was presented at the Director's Fortnight of the 2007 Cannes Festival.

MOHAMED KACIMI is an Algerian playwright and novelist. His writings include *1962*, *la Confession d'Abraham*, and *Terre sainte*.

MARJOLIJN DE JAGER has been translating Dutch and French for the past twenty years and has taught literary translation at NYU. She has been awarded various prizes for her translations, including *ForeWord* magazine's 2007 Book of the Year Award for *The Amputated Memory*, also published by the Feminist Press.

The Feminist Press is an independent nonprofit literary publisher that promotes freedom of expression and social justice. We publish exciting writing by women and men who share an activist spirit and a belief in choice and equality. Founded in 1970, we began by rescuing "lost" works by writers such as Zora Neale Hurston and Charlotte Perkins Gilman, and established our publishing program with books by American writers of diverse racial and class backgrounds. Since then we have also been bringing works from around the world to North American readers. We seek out innovative, often surprising books that tell a different story.

See our complete list of books on at **feministpress.org**, and join the Friends of FP to receive all our books at a great discount.

THE FEMINIST PRESS
AT THE CITY UNIVERSITY OF NEW YORK
FEMINISTPRESS.ORG